185 Swiss Recipes

(185 Swiss Recipes - Volume 1)

Natasha Wu

Copyright: Published in the United States by Natasha Wu/ © NATASHA WU

Published on July, 24 2020

All rights reserved. No part of this publication may be reproduced, stored in retrieval system, copied in any form or by any means, electronic, mechanical, photocopying, recording or otherwise transmitted without written permission from the publisher. Please do not participate in or encourage piracy of this material in any way. You must not circulate this book in any format. NATASHA WU does not control or direct users' actions and is not responsible for the information or content shared, harm and/or actions of the book readers.

In accordance with the U.S. Copyright Act of 1976, the scanning, uploading and electronic sharing of any part of this book without the permission of the publisher constitute unlawful piracy and theft of the author's intellectual property. If you would like to use material from the book (other than just simply for reviewing the book), prior permission must be obtained by contacting the author at author@hugecookbook.com

Thank you for your support of the author's rights.

Content

CHAPTER 1: SWISS CHEESE RECIPES 6

1. Baked Cheese Polenta With Swiss Chard ... 6
2. Cauliflower, Rice Swiss Cheese Casserole . 7
3. Cheese Omelette (Omelette Au Fromage) . 7
4. Cheese Soup (From Switzerland) 8
5. Chicken, Swiss Cheese And Stuffing Bake . 8
6. Corned Beef, Broccoli And Swiss Cheese Pockets 9
7. Crab Meat And Swiss Cheese Quiche 9
8. Easy Gourmet Swiss Mac N' Cheese 10
9. Grilled Swiss Cheese And Chicken Sandwiches 10
10. Ham And Swiss Cheese Bake 11
11. Ham And Swiss Cheese Potatoes (Crock Pot) 12
12. Ham And Swiss Cheese Quiche 12
13. Low Fat, Low Cal And Healthy Grilled Swiss Cheese 13
14. Mashed Potato And Ham Swiss Cheese Bake 13
15. Mommy's Swiss Cheese Omelette For 2 Or More 14
16. Roasted Tomato And Swiss Cheese Sandwich 14
17. Stuffed Portobella Mushrooms With Tuna Swiss Cheese 15
18. Swiss Almond Cheese Spread 15
19. Swiss Cheese Parmesan Onion Soup 16
20. Swiss Cheese Spinach Quiche 16
21. Swiss Cheese Quiche (Julia Child) 17
22. Swiss Cheese Sauce 17
23. Swiss Cheese Soup (With Variation) 18
24. Swiss Cheese Spread 18
25. Swiss Cheese And Cherry Spread 19
26. Swiss Cheese And Sausage Egg Bake 19
27. Swiss, Cheddar, And Bacon Cheese Ball .. 20
28. Swiss Nut Cheese Ball 20
29. Todays Special (chicken With Swiss Cheese And Wine) 21
30. Vegan Cheese Fondue 21
31. Vegetable Cheese Souffle 22
32. Versatile Cheese Fondue 22
33. Warm And Creamy Swiss Cheese Dip With Caraway 23

CHAPTER 2: SWISS SIDE DISH RECIPES 23

34. "gilded" Zucchini 23
35. Alplermagrone (Swiss Gruyere Cheese Pasta) 24
36. Bacon Swiss Mac And Cheese 24
37. Bacon And Swiss Scalloped Potatoes 25
38. Bacon, Swiss Chard, Potato, And Vegetable Soul Satisfying Soup 26
39. Berner Rösti 26
40. Blitva (Croatian Swiss Chard Dish) 27
41. Creamy Swiss Spinach Bake 27
42. Fried Potato Cake 28
43. Orecchiette With Swiss Chard, Tomatoes And Goat Cheese 29
44. Rachael Ray's Savory Swiss Chard 29
45. Rosti With Mushrooms 30
46. Sauerkraut Potatoes 30
47. Sauteed Swiss Chard And Corn 31
48. Sauteed Swiss Chard With Red Onions 31
49. Simply Swiss Hash Browns #5FIX 32
50. Spicy Swiss Chard With Lemon 32
51. Sweet And Sour Cabbage 33
52. Swiss Beef Crescent Ring 33
53. Swiss Chard With Chickpeas And Feta 34
54. Swiss Chard With Raisins And Pine Nuts. 34
55. Swiss Chard In Sauce Gruyere 35
56. Swiss Chard, Potato, And Chickpea Stew . 36
57. Tomatoes Fribourg Style (Tomates Fribourgeoises) 36
58. Zwiebelwähe (Swiss Onion Tart) 37

CHAPTER 3: SWISS DESSERT RECIPES 38

59. Baker's Fabulously Flawless Fudge 38
60. Baseler Leckerli (Swiss Spice Cookies) 38
61. Basler Lackerli (Swiss Spiced Honey Cookies) 39
62. Candy Cane Brunch Cakes 40
63. Chocolate Almond Crisps 41
64. Chocolate Pecan Toffee 41
65. Date And Muesli Slice 42
66. Dutch Baby With Strawberries 42
67. Frittata Of Sweet Potatoes, Swiss Chard, Peppers And Onions 43
68. Frozen Swiss Roll Ice Cream Cake 44

69. Frozen Swiss Strawberries 44
70. Geneva Pear Flan 44
71. Getränkter Zitronencake (Swiss Lemon Loaf) 45
72. Gluten Free Swiss Roll 46
73. Leckerli 46
74. Magenbrot, Soft Gingerbread 47
75. Mandel Broetli (Almond Biscuits) 48
76. Raspberry Chocolate Hazelnut Tart 48
77. Riebeles (Swiss Fried Cornmeal Cakes) 49
78. Rüebli Kuchen (Carrot Cake) 50
79. Schokoladeschaumden (Swiss Chocolate Puffs) 50
80. Springerle Cookies 51
81. Sweet Ham And Swiss Sliders 51
82. Sweet Onion And Swiss Phyllo Roll Ups . 52
83. Swiss Alps Cookies 53
84. Swiss Apple Tart Apfelwähe 53
85. Swiss Apple And Bread Dessert 54
86. Swiss Cherry Cheese Torte 55
87. Swiss Chocolate Cherry Kuchen 55
88. Swiss Chocolate Mousse 56
89. Swiss Honey Cake (Lebkuchen) 56
90. Swiss Meringues (Meringues Schalen) 57
91. Swiss Milk Toffee 57
92. Swiss Plum Kuchen 58
93. Swiss Roll With Lemon Curd Filling 59
94. Swiss Tobleronemousse 60
95. Swiss Walnut Pie (Engadiner Nusstorte Or Bündner Nusstorte) 60
96. Swiss Zug Cherry Torte (Zuger Kirschtorte) 61
97. Tangerine Cream With Brittle Topping 62
98. Totenbeinli Swiss Hazel Nut Legs 63
99. Warm Chicory Salad With Sweet Garlic, Croutons, Bacon Roqu 63
100. Zimtsterne, Cinnamon Stars 64
101. Zurich Vicarage Tart 65

CHAPTER 4: SWISS HOLIDAY EVENT RECIPES 65

102. Aussie Swiss Chicken 66
103. Fondue For Crusty French Bread 66
104. German Country Style Sourdough Rye Bread With Caraway Seeds 67
105. Grittibanzen Christmas Bread Men 67
106. Gurkensalat (Cucumber Relish Salad) 68

107. Ham Swiss Crescent Ring 68
108. Jolly Baby Swiss Spread 69
109. Marché De Noël Vin Chaud French Spiced Mulled Wine 69
110. Microwave Gruyère Fondue 70
111. Mimi's The Comeback 70
112. Mini Hot Ham Swiss Sandwiches 71
113. New Potatoes With Three Cheese Fondue 71
114. One Pot Swiss Steak With Mushrooms 72
115. Oven Baked Muesli 73
116. Potato Gratin With Apple, Pancetta And Swiss 73
117. Pretzels I 74
118. Quatre Épices French Four Spice Mix From The Auberge 74
119. Rösti (Bernese Fried Potatoes) 75
120. Savory Baked Onions With Swiss Cheese. 75
121. Schokoladen Torte (Chocolate Cake) 76
122. Smoked Ham Salad On Gruyere Potato Coins 76
123. Swiss Chard Potato Soup 77
124. Swiss Chard And Leek Gratin 78
125. Swiss Cheese Appetizer 78
126. Swiss Cheese Cranberry And Pineapple Spread 79
127. Swiss Cheese And Ham Macaroni And Cheese 79
128. Swiss Melt Mushroom Burgers 80
129. Swiss Meringue 80
130. Swiss Mocha Coffee Mix 81
131. Swiss Vegetable Casserole 81
132. Swiss White Chocolate Coffee 82
133. Tartiflette Alpine Melted Cheese, Bacon And Potato Gratin 82
134. Three Cheese Fondue With Tomato Onion Chutney 83
135. Traditional Swiss Fondue 84
136. Triple Double Trouble A.k.a. The Painkiller 84
137. White Asparagus In White Sauce 85

CHAPTER 5: AWESOME SWISS RECIPES
.... 85

138. "swiss" Round Steak With Onion Gravy .. 85
139. A Symphony Of French Chocolate Truffles 86

140. Appenzell Style Oat Soup 87
141. Après Ski Holiday Hot Chocolate With Brandy And Cream 88
142. Bacon And Swiss Cheese Dip 88
143. Bavarian Pretzel Rolls 89
144. Birchermuesli 90
145. Buendner Spinach With Smoked Bacon ... 90
146. Chocolate Fondu 91
147. Chocolate Mischief Goddess Heaven Milkshakes Of Choice 91
148. Chocolate Mousse With Raspberry Puree 92
149. Chocolate Orange Toppers 92
150. Chocolate Swiss Roll, Diabetic 93
151. Creamy Swiss Chard Pasta 94
152. Croutes Aux Champignons (Mushrooms On Toast) 94
153. Crustless Bacon, Spinach Swiss Quiche Low Carb 95
154. Crustless Swiss Chard Quiche 96
155. Deviled Ham And Swiss Cheese Spread ... 96
156. Fluffy Omelette With Ham, Spinach And Swiss Cheese 97
157. Grilled Turkey And Swiss Panini Sandwich 97
158. Ham And Cheese Rösti 98
159. Ham And Swiss Loaded Baked Potatoes .. 98
160. Karen's Swiss Steak (Stove Top, Crock Pot Or Oven) 99
161. Kings Hawaiian Ham Swiss Slider 100
162. Lighter Grilled Swiss, Ham And Asparagus Sannie 100
163. Low Fat Bircher Muesli 101
164. Lumumba (Swiss Hot Chocolate With Peppercorns) 101
165. Mushroom Swiss Veggie Burger 102
166. Omelette (Pancakes/Crepes) 102
167. Pommes De Terre Au Lard Or Speckkartoffeln (Bacon Potatoes) 103
168. Saint Moritz Martini 103
169. Sautéed Swiss Chard With Garlic 104
170. Skiers Swiss Cereal (Rainy Day Breakfast) 104
171. Spargel White Asparagus With Easy Hollandaise Sauce 105
172. Spicy Swiss Chard Or Spinach 106
173. St. Moritz Cocktail 106
174. Steamed Fish With Sour Cream Sauce 106
175. Swiss Breakfast Parfait 107
176. Swiss Cheese Bacon Smoked Almond Dip 107
177. Swiss Fondue Bread 108
178. Swiss Muesli 108
179. Swiss Spaetzle (Very Easy Homemade Noodle) 109
180. Swiss Steak In Foil 109
181. Swiss, Ham, Potato Soup 110
182. Three Colours Chocolate Crème 110
183. Two Colour Chocolate Terrine Panaché 111
184. Ww 3 Points Swiss Miss Fat Free Chocolate Fudge Pudding 111
185. Zupse Bread Swiss Bread 112

INDEX **113**
CONCLUSION **116**

Chapter 1: Swiss Cheese Recipes

***

1. Baked Cheese Polenta With Swiss Chard

Serving: 6 serving(s) | Prep: 30mins | Ready in:

Ingredients

- 2 tablespoons olive oil
- 6 garlic cloves, minced
- 8 cups chopped swiss chard, stems , leaves
- cooking spray, for pan
- The Polenta
- 1 (14 1/2 ounce) can chicken broth
- 1 1/2 cups water
- 1/2 teaspoon salt
- 1 cup cornmeal or 1 cup quick-cooking polenta
- 1 tablespoon butter
- 3 tablespoons grated parmesan cheese
- 1 cup grated mozzarella cheese
- 1/3-1/2 cup sour cream

Direction

- Heat the oil in a large skillet over medium heat; Add the garlic and cook 30 seconds, then stir in Swiss chard stems; pour in a couple tablespoons water and cover pan; cook the stems 2 minutes; Remove the cover and mix in the Swiss chard leaves; Cover the pan again and cook until the leaves wilt, about 3 minutes; Remove pan from heat and let cool, uncovered.
- Preheat the oven to 400°F; spray a 2 1/2-quart shallow baking dish with cooking spray and set aside.
- Combine the chicken broth, water and salt in a medium size saucepan and bring to a boil; reduce the heat to medium-low and SLOWLY drizzle in the cornmeal, WHISKING all the while with a wire whisk.
- Continue to cook and whisk the polenta until it is the consistency mashed potatoes, about 5 minutes; whisk in 2 tablespoons of Parmesan cheese, the 1 tablespoon butter, and the Mozzarella cheese.
- Spread HALF of the polenta into the baking dish; Spoon on Swiss chard and distribute it evenly on top of polenta; Drop on small spoonfuls of the sour cream over Swiss chard; spread it out with back of spoon.
- Spoon on the remaining polenta and spread it out; Sprinkle on the remaining tablespoon of Parmesan cheese (the casserole may be prepared to this point and refrigerated up to 24 hours in advance, bring to room temperature before baking).
- Bake the polenta for 20 to 25 minutes, or until golden on top and sizzling, DO NOT overcook it because you want to retain its creamy interior.

Nutrition Information

- Calories: 247.2
- Saturated Fat: 6.4
- Sodium: 713.5
- Total Carbohydrate: 19.6
- Protein: 9.6
- Total Fat: 15.1
- Fiber: 2.3
- Sugar: 1.6
- Cholesterol: 28.7

2. Cauliflower, Rice Swiss Cheese Casserole

Serving: 6 serving(s) | Prep: 30mins | Ready in:

Ingredients

- 4 ounces mushrooms, sliced
- 1 large onion, chopped
- 3 tablespoons butter, divided
- 1 lemon, juice of
- 1 head cauliflower, broken into florets
- 3 garlic cloves, minced
- 1 teaspoon basil
- 1/2 teaspoon salt
- 1/8 teaspoon black pepper
- 3 cups cooked brown rice
- 2 1/2 cups swiss cheese, grated
- 1/3 cup toasted walnuts, in pieces

Direction

- Preheat oven to 350°.
- To toast the walnuts, heat them in a dry pan over low heat, stirring occasionally, until they are fragrant and showing some oil. Remove from heat and let cool.
- Sauté the onion and mushrooms in 2 Tbl butter over medium heat until onion begins to soften, and mushrooms give up some of their liquid -- about 5 minutes.
- Stir in the lemon juice and sauté a minute more.
- Separately, sauté the cauliflower in 1 Tbl butter along with the garlic, basil, salt and pepper, until the cauliflower is just tender.
- Combine the onions, cauliflower, rice, Swiss cheese and toasted walnuts and mix thoroughly.
- Place in a casserole dish and bake, covered, for 30 to 40 minutes.

Nutrition Information

- Calories: 416.5
- Total Fat: 23.5
- Saturated Fat: 12.2
- Cholesterol: 56.7
- Sodium: 353
- Fiber: 5.2
- Sugar: 4.7
- Total Carbohydrate: 35.7
- Protein: 18.3

3. Cheese Omelette (Omelette Au Fromage)

Serving: 2 serving(s) | Prep: 5mins | Ready in:

Ingredients

- 4 extra large eggs
- fine salt, to taste
- fresh ground black pepper, to taste
- nutmeg, freshly ground, to taste
- 1 ounce parmesan cheese, grated
- 2 tablespoons butter
- 2 ounces gruyere cheese, grated

Direction

- Break the eggs into a bowl.
- Season to taste with salt, pepper, and nutmeg.
- Add Parmesan cheese.
- Beat the eggs with a fork until just mixed.
- Heat a large frying pan over medium heat.
- Add the butter and allow it to melt and color slightly.
- Add the beaten eggs.
- Use the flat side of the fork to stir the eggs until they start to set.
- Smooth the top and leave the eggs to cook.
- Add the Gruyere cheese over the surface.
- Fold the omelet into thirds and flip it onto a heated serving plate.

Nutrition Information

- Calories: 450.5
- Cholesterol: 564.9
- Protein: 28.6

- Total Fat: 36.3
- Saturated Fat: 18.7
- Fiber: 0
- Total Carbohydrate: 1.6
- Sodium: 556.2
- Sugar: 1.1

4. Cheese Soup (From Switzerland)

Serving: 4 serving(s) | Prep: 15mins | Ready in:

Ingredients

- 1/2 cup oatmeal
- 1 teaspoon salt
- 1/2 cup butter
- 4 -6 cups water (or consomme)
- 2 potatoes, peeled and cut into thin slices
- 2 cups grated emmenthaler cheese
- 1 dash nutmeg (optional)

Direction

- Saute the oatmeal and salt in half the butter until golden brown.
- Add the water; bring to a boil. Cook over low heat, stirring occasionally and adding water if necessary, until the oatmeal is cooked into a gruel. This will take about 90 minutes.
- Add the sliced potatoes. Cook about 30 minutes until they are tender.
- Stir in the grated cheese, remaining butter and nutmeg if desired. Add additional hot water if it's too thick.

Nutrition Information

- Calories: 324.3
- Sodium: 756.4
- Cholesterol: 61
- Total Fat: 23.8
- Saturated Fat: 14.7
- Fiber: 3.3

- Sugar: 1
- Total Carbohydrate: 25.4
- Protein: 4

5. Chicken, Swiss Cheese And Stuffing Bake

Serving: 5 , 5 serving(s) | Prep: 20mins | Ready in:

Ingredients

- 5 boneless skinless chicken breasts
- 5 slices swiss cheese (you can also try with Pepper jack, Monterey...)
- 1 (10 1/2 ounce) can cream of onion soup
- 1/4 cup white wine (you can substitute for milk if you prefer)
- seasoned stuffing mix (we recommend garlic and herbs, but you can use the plain one as well)
- 1/4 cup butter
- salt and pepper

Direction

- 1. Preheat your oven to 350 F (175 C). Grease a casserole dish and season your chicken breasts.
- 2. In a mixing bowl, mix the white wine (or the milk) with the can of cream of onion soup. Add a couple of spoonfuls of the soup and wine mixture to the casserole and spread it. Arrange your chicken breasts and cover each one of them with a slice of the cheese.
- 3. Pour the rest of the soup and wine mixture over the chicken and the cheese.
- 4. Pour the stuffing mix over the casserole and sprinkle it with the butter.
- 5. Cover the dish with foil and bake for 35 minutes. Remove the foil and bake for 10-15 more minutes or until golden brown.
- Pro tip: If you're going to freeze this casserole, it's better not to add the stuffing and add it whenever you're going to eat it. That way the bread won't get soggy while it thaws. In any

case, serve over rice or with a side of steamed green beans.

Nutrition Information

- Calories: 384.4
- Protein: 34
- Total Carbohydrate: 8
- Cholesterol: 132.8
- Total Fat: 22.6
- Saturated Fat: 12.2
- Sodium: 651.8
- Fiber: 0.2
- Sugar: 2.7

6. Corned Beef, Broccoli And Swiss Cheese Pockets

Serving: 4 pockets, 1 serving(s) | Prep: 5mins | Ready in:

Ingredients

- 1 (10 ounce) canrefrigerated prepared pizza crust
- 1/2 lb corned beef, cut into 1/2 inch cubes
- 1 tablespoon butter
- 1/2 chopped onion
- 1 1/2 cups frozen chopped broccoli, defrosted
- 1 cup shredded swiss cheese
- 1/4 teaspoon pepper
- 8 teaspoons thousand island dressing

Direction

- Heat oven to 425 degrees. In medium non-stick skillet, heat butter until hot. Add onion; cook and stir 2 to 3 minutes or until tender. Remove from heat; add corned beef, broccoli, cheese and pepper; mix well.
- On ungreased baking sheet, unroll pizza dough; cut into quarters. Flatten each quarter into 6 x 5-inch rectangle; spread each with 2 teaspoons dressing to within 1-inch from edges.
- Place equal amounts of corned beef mixture in center of each. Bring together 2 opposite corners of dough, pinching to seal. Loosely close straight edges of dough to form diamond-shaped sandwiches. (Not necessary to seal edges completely).
- Bake in 425 degree oven 11 to 13 minutes or until golden brown.

Nutrition Information

- Calories: 1319.2
- Fiber: 8.3
- Protein: 78
- Total Fat: 99.8
- Saturated Fat: 43.1
- Cholesterol: 363
- Sodium: 3275.6
- Sugar: 13.1
- Total Carbohydrate: 30

7. Crab Meat And Swiss Cheese Quiche

Serving: 8-10 serving(s) | Prep: 5mins | Ready in:

Ingredients

- 1/2 cup milk
- 1/2 cup mayonnaise
- 1/3 cup chopped green onion (scallions)
- 2 tablespoons flour
- 1 egg (optional)
- 12 ounces swiss cheese or 12 ounces baby swiss cheese, cubed
- 1 (12 ounce) candrained crabmeat
- fresh parsley (to garnish) (optional)

Direction

- Preheat oven to 350 degrees.
- Mix first 5 ingredients thoroughly in large bowl Mix in cubed Swiss or Baby Swiss Cheese.

- Mix in drained crab meat.
- Pour mix into an unbaked pie shell.
- Cook for 30-45 minutes at 350 degrees.
- Add parsley or other garnish if desired.
- Serve warm.

Nutrition Information

- Calories: 272.8
- Fiber: 0.2
- Total Carbohydrate: 8.3
- Cholesterol: 62.9
- Protein: 20.1
- Saturated Fat: 8.7
- Sodium: 549.5
- Sugar: 1.6
- Total Fat: 17.6

8. Easy Gourmet Swiss Mac N' Cheese

Serving: 8-10 serving(s) | Prep: 20mins | Ready in:

Ingredients

- 1/3 lb bacon, cut in 1-inch pieces
- 1 tablespoon oil
- 1 large onion, cut into 3/8-inch rings
- 2 tablespoons water
- 1 (12 ounce) container cheese spread, Swiss and Almond flavor, Merkt's preferred
- 1 cup milk
- 1/2 lb mozzarella cheese, finely shredded
- 1 lb wide egg noodles

Direction

- Heat 8 cups water to boil for noodles. When water boils, add noodles and cook about 1 minute less than package directs. Drain.
- Put oil and onion into saucepan. Stir to coat onion with oil. Add water, cover and sweat the onions over medium-low heat until they wilt and become sweet. Stir occasionally. Do not allow onions to brown.
- Fry bacon in large deep pot over medium heat until golden. Spoon onto paper towels to drain. Set aside.
- Drain the bacon fat from the pot, but do not wash.
- Add milk to bacon cooking pot and heat to simmer.
- Add cheese spread and whisk until cheese melts and mixture is smooth.
- Add mozzarella. Stir in figure 8 pattern (keeps it from balling up on the spoon) until cheese melts and mixture is smooth.
- Add onions to cheese mixture and stir gently.
- Add noodles and turn until well coated.
- Pour into serving dish.
- Top with bacon and serve.

Nutrition Information

- Calories: 556.2
- Fiber: 2.1
- Total Carbohydrate: 48.4
- Protein: 24.7
- Sodium: 1053.8
- Saturated Fat: 13.8
- Sugar: 2.2
- Cholesterol: 110.8
- Total Fat: 29.2

9. Grilled Swiss Cheese And Chicken Sandwiches

Serving: 2 serving(s) | Prep: 30mins | Ready in:

Ingredients

- 1 1/2 tablespoons unsalted butter
- 1 whole boneless skinless chicken breast (about 3/4 pound)
- 3 tablespoons mayonnaise
- 1 tablespoon good quality ketchup
- 4 slices rye bread (thick slices)

- 4 slices swiss cheese, cut to fit the bread
- 2 small whole sweet pickles, sliced thin, plus
- 2 whole pickles (to garnish)
- 2 slices red onions (thin slices)
- 1 large egg
- 2 tablespoons milk

Direction

- In a small, heavy skillet heat 1/2 tablespoons of the butter over moderately high heat until the foam subsides. In it, saute the chicken, turning it once, for 12 to 15 minutes, or it is springy to the touch and just cooked through, and on a work surface shred the chicken.
- In a small bowl combine well the mayonnaise, the ketchup, and salt and pepper to taste, divide the mixture among the bread slices, spreading it, and top it with the Swiss cheese. Divide the pickle and onion slices between 2 of the half-sandwiches, top them with the chicken, and cover the chicken, with the remaining half-sandwiches.
- In a small shallow disk whisk together the egg, milk, and salt and pepper to taste, press each sandwich together firmly, and dip the sandwiches, one at a time, in the egg mixture, turning them to coat them thoroughly. In a heavy skillet heat 1/2 tablespoons of the remaining butter over moderate heat until the foam subsides and in it cook the sandwiches, covered, for 4 minutes or until the undersides are a golden brown. Transfer the sandwiches to plates, halve them with a serrated knife, and garnish them with the whole pickles, cut lengthwise into fan shapes.

Nutrition Information

- Calories: 754.6
- Total Fat: 39.9
- Saturated Fat: 18.8
- Fiber: 4.8
- Cholesterol: 250.8
- Sodium: 1589.1
- Sugar: 10.6
- Total Carbohydrate: 48.1
- Protein: 50.3

10. Ham And Swiss Cheese Bake

Serving: 8 serving(s) | Prep: 14mins | Ready in:

Ingredients

- 2 cups Bisquick
- 1/3 cup honey mustard
- 1/3 cup milk
- 2 cups cubed cooked ham
- 4 medium green onions, sliced
- 1/4 cup chopped red bell pepper
- 1/4 cup sour cream
- 1 cup shredded swiss cheese

Direction

- Heat oven to 450.
- Grease bottom and sides of rectangular pan, 13x9x2 inches, with shortening. Stir Bisquick, mustard and milk until soft dough forms; press on bottom of pan. Bake 8 to 10 minutes or until crust is golden brown.
- Mix ham, onions, bell pepper and sour cream; spread over crust. Sprinkle with cheese.
- Bake uncovered 5 to 6 minutes or until mixture is hot and cheese is melted.

Nutrition Information

- Calories: 325.3
- Sugar: 6.4
- Total Carbohydrate: 25.4
- Protein: 16
- Total Fat: 17.4
- Fiber: 1
- Saturated Fat: 7
- Sodium: 472
- Cholesterol: 49.9

11. Ham And Swiss Cheese Potatoes (Crock Pot)

Serving: 6 serving(s) | Prep: 10mins | Ready in:

Ingredients

- 0.5 (32 ounce) package French fries (frozen, straight cut)
- 1 onion, chopped
- 2 garlic cloves, minced
- 1 1/4 cups ham (fully cooked, cubed)
- 1 cup swiss cheese, shredded
- 1 (10 ounce) can cream of potato soup
- 1/2 cup ricotta cheese
- 1/8 teaspoon pepper
- 1/2 teaspoon dried marjoram
- 1 1/2 cups frozen peas (thawed)
- 1/4 cup parmesan cheese, grated

Direction

- In 3 1/2 quart slow cooker, combine potatoes, onions, garlic, ham, Swiss cheese and mix well.
- In medium bowl, combine soup, ricotta cheese, pepper and marjoram, blend and then pour over the potato mixture.
- Cover and cook on low 8-9 hours or until potatoes are tender.
- Stir in peas and Parmesan cheese, cover and cook on high 30-40 min or until peas are hot.
- Serve immediately.

Nutrition Information

- Calories: 368.5
- Total Fat: 14.6
- Cholesterol: 48.2
- Protein: 21.6
- Saturated Fat: 7.2
- Sodium: 1143.4
- Fiber: 5.5
- Sugar: 5.5
- Total Carbohydrate: 37.7

12. Ham And Swiss Cheese Quiche

Serving: 6-8 serving(s) | Prep: 15mins | Ready in:

Ingredients

- 2 tablespoons flour
- 8 ounces natural swiss cheese
- 2 cups half-and-half
- 4 eggs
- 3/4 cup ham, chopped
- 1 tablespoon onion, chopped
- 1 tablespoon green pepper, chopped
- 1/2 teaspoon salt
- pepper, to taste
- 1 pie crust, deep dish (bought, as I do, or homemade)

Direction

- Toss together the flour and Swiss cheese.
- Mix in the half and half.
- Slightly beat the eggs, with a fork, and stir into mixture.
- Mix in the ham, onion, and green pepper.
- Season with salt and pepper.
- Pour into a large pie crust.
- Bake at 375 degrees for 50-60 minutes.

Nutrition Information

- Calories: 485.4
- Total Fat: 34.1
- Saturated Fat: 16.4
- Total Carbohydrate: 21.7
- Cholesterol: 214.7
- Protein: 22.8
- Sodium: 767.4
- Fiber: 1.2
- Sugar: 1.1

13. Low Fat, Low Cal And Healthy Grilled Swiss Cheese

Serving: 1 sandwich, 1 serving(s) | Prep: 2mins | Ready in:

Ingredients

- 1 slice of kraft singles 2% low-fat swiss cheese (reduced fat)
- 2 slices white bread
- 2 teaspoons butter
- 1 teaspoon flax seed

Direction

- 1. Put the cheese slice on the bread.
- 2. Spread the flaxseed on the cheese.
- 3. Cover with the other slice of bread.
- 4. Put 1 teaspoon of butter on each bred slice. Pour in a panini-press preferably or in a skillet.

Nutrition Information

- Calories: 268.6
- Cholesterol: 29.9
- Protein: 12.5
- Fiber: 2.1
- Saturated Fat: 6.2
- Sodium: 468.3
- Sugar: 2.6
- Total Carbohydrate: 27.2
- Total Fat: 12.1

14. Mashed Potato And Ham Swiss Cheese Bake

Serving: 4-6 serving(s) | Prep: 40mins | Ready in:

Ingredients

- 7 large russet potatoes, peeled
- 1/4 cup melted butter (no substitutions)
- 1 -2 teaspoon seasoning salt (or to taste or use white salt)
- black pepper
- 1 pinch nutmeg
- 2 tablespoons whipping cream or 2 tablespoons buttermilk
- 1 1/2 cups swiss cheese, finely diced
- 1 1/2 cups cubed cooked ham
- 3 green onions, finely chopped
- 3 large eggs
- 1/2 cup milk
- 1/4 cup parmesan cheese (optional)
- paprika

Direction

- Set oven to 375 degrees.
- Butter a 2-quart casserole dish.
- Cook the potatoes in boiling water until fork-tender; drain and place in a bowl.
- Mash potatoes then add in butter, salt, pepper, pinch nutmeg and whipping cream; mix until well combined.
- Spoon about two-thirds of the potato mixture on the bottom and up the sides of the prepared baking dish; set aside (this can be done up to a day in advance, covered and refrigerated).
- In a bowl combine the shredded Swiss cheese, cubed ham and green onions; spoon the mixture into the potato-lined dish.
- In a bowl beat eggs with milk; pour over the ham/cheese mixture.
- Spoon (or pipe) the remaining potato mixture over the top.
- Sprinkle with Parmesan cheese (if using) then paprika.
- Bake for 35-40 minutes or until golden brown.
- Let stand about 10 minutes before serving.

Nutrition Information

- Calories: 995.3
- Total Fat: 39.9
- Saturated Fat: 21.5
- Sodium: 300.7
- Sugar: 6.2

- Total Carbohydrate: 117.8
- Fiber: 14.5
- Cholesterol: 288.5
- Protein: 43.7

15. Mommy's Swiss Cheese Omelette For 2 Or More

Serving: 2 serving(s) | Prep: 5mins | Ready in:

Ingredients

- 3 eggs
- 1 tablespoon water
- 1 tablespoon butter
- nonstick cooking spray
- 1 pinch salt
- 1 pinch pepper
- 1/2 cup swiss cheese, shredded
- 2 bagels

Direction

- Beat eggs with water and add pepper to mix.
- Spray Large Omelette Pan with non-stick spray while cold.
- Melt butter in large omelette pan over medium heat-be careful not to burn the butter.
- Pour egg mix into pan and swirl around to cover-lower heat to low.
- Keep swirling pan so that egg evenly cooks over the low heat- be careful not to overcook or brown the bottom too much.
- When eggs are almost cooked through (top is still soft) sprinkle cheese over the top.
- Put lid onto pan and turn off heat - let this sit for about 1-2 minutes until cheese melts and eggs puff up.
- Sprinkle salt lightly on top.
- Fold omelette over and cut in half.
- Serve over a hot bagel (open face).

Nutrition Information

- Calories: 450.5
- Total Fat: 21.5
- Saturated Fat: 10.9
- Sugar: 0.6
- Total Carbohydrate: 38.8
- Protein: 24
- Sodium: 655
- Fiber: 1.6
- Cholesterol: 319.1

16. Roasted Tomato And Swiss Cheese Sandwich

Serving: 1 sandwich, 1 serving(s) | Prep: 5mins | Ready in:

Ingredients

- 1 tomatoes
- oregano
- basil
- salt
- pepper
- olive oil
- 2 slices bread
- 1 tablespoon mayonnaise
- 1 slice swiss cheese

Direction

- Slice tomato fairly thin, between a quarter and half an inch. Place on parchment and sheet pan, drizzle with olive oil, sprinkle salt, pepper, oregano and basil and place under maxi broil in middle of the oven (same position that you would use to bake anything else).
- After about 5 minutes, flip tomato slices, drizzle more olive oil and sprinkle more pepper, oregano and basil. Bake about 5 more minutes.
- Toast the bread, spread on mayo, and put 2 or 3 slices of tomato on one slice and Swiss cheese on top of tomato. Grind a little more pepper and place under broiler to melt cheese.

- Place other slice of bread on top and enjoy!

Nutrition Information

- Calories: 318.9
- Sodium: 419.9
- Fiber: 2.7
- Sugar: 6.7
- Protein: 12.6
- Total Fat: 14.6
- Cholesterol: 29.6
- Saturated Fat: 6.1
- Total Carbohydrate: 35.1

17. Stuffed Portobella Mushrooms With Tuna Swiss Cheese

Serving: 4 serving(s) | Prep: 25mins | Ready in:

Ingredients

- 4 large portabella mushrooms
- 7 ounces tuna in brine, drained
- 2 tablespoons mayonnaise
- 2 ounces swiss cheese, grated
- cayenne pepper

Direction

- Top large Portobello mushrooms with a mixture of the tuna mayonnaise. Top with the Swiss cheese and a sprinkle of cayenne pepper.
- Place onto a greased baking tray and cook under a medium broiler until the cheese has melted begins to brown.

Nutrition Information

- Calories: 199.5
- Total Fat: 10.8
- Saturated Fat: 3.7
- Sugar: 2.8
- Total Carbohydrate: 5.8
- Sodium: 263
- Fiber: 1.1
- Cholesterol: 23.9
- Protein: 20.1

18. Swiss Almond Cheese Spread

Serving: 2 1/2 cups | Prep: 10mins | Ready in:

Ingredients

- 1 (8 ounce) package cream cheese, softened
- 1 1/2 cups shredded swiss cheese
- 1/2 cup sliced almonds, toasted, divided
- 1/3 cup mayonnaise
- 2 tablespoons sliced green onions
- 1/8 teaspoon pepper
- 1/8 teaspoon ground nutmeg

Direction

- In a small mixing bowl, beat the cream cheese until smooth.
- Stir in the Swiss cheese, 1/3 cup almonds, mayonnaise, onions, pepper and nutmeg.
- Spoon onto a lightly greased pie plate.
- Bake at 350 degrees F for 14-15 minutes or until heated through.
- Sprinkle with remaining almonds. Serve warm with crackers.

Nutrition Information

- Calories: 793.7
- Total Fat: 69.5
- Cholesterol: 167.6
- Protein: 28.6
- Saturated Fat: 33.7
- Sodium: 616.5
- Fiber: 2.4
- Sugar: 4.1
- Total Carbohydrate: 17.5

19. Swiss Cheese Parmesan Onion Soup

Serving: 6 serving(s) | Prep: 15mins | Ready in:

Ingredients

- 6 large onions, thinly sliced
- 4 tablespoons butter
- 1 teaspoon sugar
- 1 tablespoon flour
- 1 cup dry white wine
- 1 quart beef stock
- 6 large croutons
- 2 cups grated swiss cheese
- 1/2 cup grated parmesan cheese

Direction

- Preheat oven to 325°.
- In heavy bottom pan, slowly brown onions, butter and sugar until onions are dark brown, 30 minutes. With wooden spoon, scrape brown off the bottom of the pan occasionally.
- Add flour and cook, stirring, for 2 or 3 minutes.
- Add wine and cook for 2-3 minutes more.
- Add beef stick; simmer partially covered for 1 hour.
- To serve, place crouton on top of each bowl of soup (6 bowls).
- Cover generously with Swiss cheese and sprinkle with the Parmesan.
- Bake covered, for 15 minutes then uncover, bake another 10 minutes.
- Serve warmed and enjoy!

Nutrition Information

- Calories: 354.8
- Sodium: 779.1
- Protein: 16.4
- Total Fat: 20.6
- Fiber: 2.1
- Sugar: 8.1
- Total Carbohydrate: 20.2
- Cholesterol: 60.8
- Saturated Fat: 12.9

20. Swiss Cheese Spinach Quiche

Serving: 1 Quiche, 2-4 serving(s) | Prep: 25mins | Ready in:

Ingredients

- pastry dough, for one single crust pie (store bought or homemade)
- 4 slices bacon, diced
- 1/4 cup chopped onion
- 1/4 cup chopped sweet red pepper
- 1 (10 ounce) package frozen chopped spinach, thawed and squeezed dry
- 4 eggs (or 2 cups egg substitute)
- 1/2 cup cottage cheese
- 1/4 cup shredded swiss cheese
- 1/2 teaspoon dried oregano
- 1/4 teaspoon dried parsley flakes
- 1/4 teaspoon salt
- 1/4 teaspoon pepper, and
- 1/4 teaspoon paprika
- 6 tablespoons sour cream

Direction

- On a lightly floured surface, unroll pastry and transfer to a 9-inch pie plate.
- Trim pastry to 1/2 inch beyond the edge of the plate and flute edges.
- Line unpricked pastry with a double thickness of heavy duty aluminum foil.
- Bake at 450 for 8 minutes, remove foil and bake for another 5 minutes.
- Cool on a wire rack and reduce the oven to 350.
- In a small skillet cook the bacon, onions and red pepper until the veggies are tender and drain.
- Stir in the spinach.
- Spoon spinach mixture into pastry.

- In a small bowl, combine the eggs, cottage cheese, Swiss cheese and seasonings.
- Pour over spinach mixture.
- Bake for 35 - 40 minutes or until a knife inserted near center comes out clean.
- Let rest for 10 minutes before cutting.
- Serve with sour cream.

Nutrition Information

- Calories: 596.6
- Cholesterol: 490
- Total Fat: 45.2
- Sugar: 4.1
- Total Carbohydrate: 14.5
- Protein: 35.2
- Saturated Fat: 18.9
- Sodium: 1172.4
- Fiber: 5.3

21. Swiss Cheese Quiche (Julia Child)

Serving: 4-6 serving(s) | Prep: 15mins | Ready in:

Ingredients

- 3 eggs (or 2 eggs and 2 egg yolks)
- whipping cream, half and half or milk
- 1/2 teaspoon salt
- 1 pinch pepper
- 1 pinch nutmeg
- 1/2-1 cup grated swiss cheese
- 1 -2 tablespoon butter, cut into pea-sized dots
- 8 inches pastry shells, partly cooked

Direction

- To partly bake the pastry shell:
- Bake in middle of oven at 400 degrees F. for 8-9 minutes.
- For filling:
- Preheat oven to 375 degrees F. Place oven rack in upper third of oven.
- Beat eggs.
- Add enough cream (or milk or cream-milk combination) so that eggs and cream measure 1 1/2 cups total.
- Add salt, nutmeg and pepper; mix through.
- Stir in cheese. Check seasoning.
- Pour into pastry shell and distribute butter pieces on top. Place on baking sheet.
- Bake 25-30 minutes or till puffed and browned.
- Slide quiche onto a hot platter and serve.

Nutrition Information

- Calories: 342.8
- Total Fat: 24.2
- Fiber: 0.7
- Sugar: 0.6
- Saturated Fat: 8.8
- Sodium: 606.4
- Total Carbohydrate: 20
- Cholesterol: 178.7
- Protein: 10.9

22. Swiss Cheese Sauce

Serving: 5 cups (approx) | Prep: 5mins | Ready in:

Ingredients

- 3 tablespoons butter
- 3 tablespoons flour
- 3 cups half-and-half cream (or use full-fat milk)
- 2 1/4 cups grated swiss cheese
- 1 teaspoon Worcestershire sauce
- Tabasco sauce or louisanna hot sauce
- salt and pepper

Direction

- In a heavy-bottomed medium saucepan melt butter over medium heat.
- Blend/whisk in flour; cook whisking 1 minute.

- Reduce heat to medium-low and slowly add in the half and half cream, stirring until thickened.
- Add in the Swiss cheese, Worcestershire sauce and hot pepper sauce to taste; mix with a wooden spoon until the cheese has melted.
- Season with salt and pepper.

Nutrition Information

- Calories: 452.4
- Total Fat: 37.2
- Fiber: 0.1
- Total Carbohydrate: 12.7
- Cholesterol: 116.8
- Saturated Fat: 23.4
- Sodium: 213.1
- Sugar: 1
- Protein: 17.9

23. Swiss Cheese Soup (With Variation)

Serving: 6 serving(s) | Prep: 10mins | Ready in:

Ingredients

- 1 1/2 cups shallots, finely chopped
- 3 garlic cloves, minced
- 2 tablespoons butter
- 1 1/2 cups chicken broth
- 1/2 teaspoon caraway seed
- 1/8 teaspoon salt
- 1/8 teaspoon black pepper
- 1/8 teaspoon ground nutmeg
- 1 1/2 cups light cream or 1 1/2 cups milk
- 3 tablespoons all-purpose flour
- 1 1/2 cups emmenthaler cheese, shredded (6 oz)
- For Swiss Cheese-Cabbage Soup Variation add an additional
- 1/2 cup light cream or 1/2 cup milk
- 2 cups cabbage, coarsely chopped
- 1/2 cup cooked rice

Direction

- In a large saucepan cook the shallots and garlic in hot butter till the onion is tender, but not brown. Stir in the chicken broth, caraway seed, salt, pepper, and ground nutmeg. Bring to a boil; reduce heat. Cover; simmer for 15 minutes.
- Combine the light cream or milk and flour (increase the milk or light cream by 1/2 cup if adding the cabbage and rice); add to the mixture in the saucepan. If adding the cabbage and rice, do this now as well. Cook and stir until thickened and bubbly. Cook and stir 1 minute more.
- Reduce heat. Add the cheese; cook and stir until the cheese is partially melted. Serve immediately with crusty white bread, if desired.

Nutrition Information

- Calories: 271.3
- Total Fat: 19.8
- Sugar: 1.1
- Total Carbohydrate: 19.2
- Cholesterol: 63
- Protein: 5.6
- Saturated Fat: 12.2
- Sodium: 310.3
- Fiber: 0.8

24. Swiss Cheese Spread

Serving: 2 cups, 25 serving(s) | Prep: 5mins | Ready in:

Ingredients

- 2 cups shredded swiss cheese
- 3 tablespoons sour cream
- 2 tablespoons minced onions
- 4 slices crisply cooked bacon, crumbled

- 1/2 teaspoon salt
- 1/2 teaspoon garlic powder

Direction

- Combine all ingredients; beat until smooth and of a spreading consistency. Chill.

Nutrition Information

- Calories: 43.4
- Cholesterol: 10
- Total Fat: 3.2
- Saturated Fat: 1.9
- Sodium: 93.5
- Fiber: 0
- Sugar: 0.2
- Total Carbohydrate: 0.7
- Protein: 2.9

25. Swiss Cheese And Cherry Spread

Serving: 2 cups | Prep: 10mins | Ready in:

Ingredients

- 12 ounces shredded swiss cheese (3 cups)
- 1/4 cup butter
- 1/2 cup dried tart cherry (can use the dried cran-cherries)
- 1/2 cup mayonnaise
- 2 teaspoons Dijon mustard
- 1/2 cup finely chopped green onion

Direction

- Bring cheese and butter to room temperature. Meanwhile, snip cherries and cover with boiling water and let stand 10 minutes.
- Drain well; pat cherries dry with paper towels and set aside.
- Place cheese, butter, mayo and mustard in a food-processor bowl.
- Cover and process till combined.
- Stir in cherries and green onions; cover and refrigerate.
- Serve with crackers or cocktail breads (rye or whole wheat is great).
- Makes about 2 cups.

Nutrition Information

- Calories: 1109.6
- Sodium: 968.9
- Sugar: 10
- Total Carbohydrate: 30.1
- Protein: 47.6
- Total Fat: 90.2
- Fiber: 1.4
- Cholesterol: 232.8
- Saturated Fat: 47.7

26. Swiss Cheese And Sausage Egg Bake

Serving: 8 serving(s) | Prep: 15mins | Ready in:

Ingredients

- 1 lb pork sausage, browned and drained
- 6 ounces sliced fresh mushrooms
- 1/4 cup green onion, chopped
- 1/2 cup chopped fresh parsley
- 2 1/2 cups grated swiss cheese
- 1 1/4 cups baking mix
- 12 large eggs
- 1 cup milk
- 1 1/4 teaspoons salt
- 1/2 teaspoon pepper
- paprika

Direction

- Butter a 13 x 9-inch baking dish. Spread sausage as first layer; scatter mushrooms, green onions and tomatoes over sausage. Next layer on parsley; top with grated cheese.

- In a large electric mixer bowl, beat together baking mix and milk until smooth. Add eggs, salt and pepper; beat on slow speed until combined. Pour over sausage mixture. Sprinkle lightly with paprika. Bake in 350 degree oven 30 to 35 minutes or until knife inserted in center comes out clean. Cut into squares to serve.

Nutrition Information

- Calories: 518.4
- Cholesterol: 393.8
- Protein: 30.5
- Total Fat: 36
- Saturated Fat: 14.8
- Fiber: 0.9
- Total Carbohydrate: 17
- Sodium: 1152.1
- Sugar: 3.7

27. Swiss, Cheddar, And Bacon Cheese Ball

Serving: 4 balls | Prep: 10mins | Ready in:

Ingredients

- 1 (8 ounce) package cheddar cheese
- 1 (8 ounce) package cream cheese
- 8 ounces of freshly grated swiss cheese
- 1 1/2 ounces bacon bits (more or less to taste)
- Club crackers

Direction

- Mix the cheddar cheese, cream cheese, and Swiss cheese thoroughly and then sprinkle in the bacon bits and mix more.
- When thoroughly mixed, use hands to form balls.
- The recipe should make about four good sized balls.

- Refrigerate for one to two hours until cheese has better consistency.
- Store in ziplock bags if not using immediately as they keep for several days.

Nutrition Information

- Calories: 699.8
- Sodium: 876.3
- Sugar: 1.2
- Saturated Fat: 36
- Fiber: 0
- Total Carbohydrate: 5.4
- Cholesterol: 185.8
- Protein: 37.6
- Total Fat: 58.8

28. Swiss Nut Cheese Ball

Serving: 1 24 ounce ball | Prep: 15mins | Ready in:

Ingredients

- 8 ounces sharp cheddar cheese, shredded (I used a shredded cheddar or mozzarella mix)
- 8 ounces swiss cheese, shredded
- 1 (8 ounce) package cream cheese
- 1/3 cup sour cream
- 2 teaspoons Worcestershire sauce
- 1/2 teaspoon paprika
- 1/2 teaspoon garlic salt
- 1/4 teaspoon black pepper
- 1/3 cup finely chopped nuts (walnuts or pecans are good, I haven't tried toasted but I bet that would be good)
- 1/4 cup fresh chives, chopped (optional- you may also use chopped fresh parsley, or fresh thyme)

Direction

- Place cheddar, Swiss, and cream cheese, sour cream, Worcestershire sauce, paprika, black pepper, and garlic salt in a medium bowl.

- Place in a food processor and pulse until well blended.
- In bowl, place nuts and chives, if using. Stir to mix.
- Shape mixture into a ball, roll in the chopped nuts and chives (if using).
- Wrap in waxed paper or plastic wrap and refrigerate until serving time.
- Serve with raw vegetables or crackers.

Nutrition Information

- Calories: 2997.1
- Total Carbohydrate: 43
- Cholesterol: 737.3
- Protein: 141.6
- Total Fat: 255.1
- Sodium: 3056.2
- Fiber: 5.1
- Sugar: 17.8
- Saturated Fat: 144.2

29. Todays Special (chicken With Swiss Cheese And Wine)

Serving: 4-8 serving(s) | Prep: 10mins | Ready in:

Ingredients

- 4 -8 boneless skinless chicken breasts
- 4 -8 slices thick swiss cheese
- 1/2 cup white wine
- 1 can cream of chicken soup (2 if using eight breasts)
- 1 package herb stuffing mix (crumbled not cubed)
- 1/2 cup butter, melted

Direction

- In lightly greased baking dish, lay out chicken breasts.
- Put 1 slice of Swiss cheese on each breast.
- Mix together wine and soup thoroughly.
- Pour soup mixture over chicken evenly.
- Sprinkle stuffing mix over top covering all chicken.
- Drizzle melted butter over stuffing.
- Bake uncovered at 350 for 45 minutes.
- Enjoy!

Nutrition Information

- Calories: 696
- Protein: 41.5
- Fiber: 1.4
- Total Carbohydrate: 40.1
- Cholesterol: 161.7
- Total Fat: 38.1
- Saturated Fat: 21.5
- Sodium: 1470.6
- Sugar: 4.6

30. Vegan Cheese Fondue

Serving: 3 cups, 4 serving(s) | Prep: 10mins | Ready in:

Ingredients

- 2 cups white wine (or 1 cup rice vinegar plus one cup water)
- 1 cup water
- 1/2 cup nutritional yeast flakes
- 1/3 cup quick-cooking rolled oats
- 1/4 cup tahini
- 4 tablespoons arrowroot or 4 tablespoons cornstarch
- 2 tablespoons fresh lemon juice
- 2 tablespoons onion powder
- 1 teaspoon salt
- 2 tablespoons Dijon mustard
- 1/8 teaspoon white pepper

Direction

- Put all of the ingredients into a blender. Blend for a few minutes. Ensure that the oats are

- ground until fine. You are aiming for a smooth consistency.
- Pour this mixture into a heavy-based saucepan. Bring to the boil while stirring constantly.
- Reduce heat to low and simmer for a few minutes. Continue to stir until the mixture turns thick and smooth.
- Prepare the fondue pot (rub with garlic and or grease with some olive oil. Pour in the vegan fondue and keep warm in the usual fashion for fondue.
- Provide crusty bread and some veggies like broccoli, mushrooms, etc.

Nutrition Information

- Calories: 332.7
- Sodium: 700.6
- Fiber: 9.6
- Cholesterol: 0
- Protein: 14.1
- Total Fat: 9.8
- Saturated Fat: 1.4
- Sugar: 1.7
- Total Carbohydrate: 32.2

31. Vegetable Cheese Souffle

Serving: 6 serving(s) | Prep: 10mins | Ready in:

Ingredients

- 1/4 cup butter
- 1/4 cup flour
- 1/2 teaspoon salt
- 1/4 teaspoon cayenne pepper
- 1 cup milk
- 8 ounces grated sharp cheddar cheese
- 3 egg yolks
- 6-8 sliced mushrooms
- 2 tablespoons diced red bell peppers
- 1/2 cup diced broccoli or 1/2 cup asparagus, tips
- 2 teaspoons olive oil
- 6 egg whites
- confectioners' sugar

Direction

- Preheat oven to 450°F.
- To Make Roux: Melt butter, then blend in flour, salt, and cayenne pepper. Add milk all at once. Cook over medium heat until mixture thickens and bubbles. Remove from heat. Add cheese, and stir until melted.
- Beat egg yolks in a separate bowl until thick and lemon colored. Slowly add to cheese mixture, stirring constantly. Reserve, cover and keep warm.
- Sauté mushrooms, red peppers, and broccoli or asparagus tips in olive oil, and reserve.
- Beat egg whites to stiff peaks.
- In a mixing bowl, add 2 cups roux to vegetables and fold in egg whites.
- Pour into an ungreased souffle dish.
- Bake in a hot water bath for 15-20 minutes or until "top hat" is slightly brown.
- Sprinkle with confectioners' sugar and serve immediately.

Nutrition Information

- Calories: 327.8
- Sugar: 1.1
- Total Carbohydrate: 8.2
- Protein: 17
- Saturated Fat: 14.7
- Sodium: 565
- Fiber: 0.6
- Cholesterol: 160.1
- Total Fat: 25.4

32. Versatile Cheese Fondue

Serving: 4-6 serving(s) | Prep: 5mins | Ready in:

Ingredients

- 1 lb grated swiss cheese
- 2 teaspoons flour
- 1/2 teaspoon salt
- 14 ounces cream cheese, softened
- 1 1/2 teaspoons Dijon mustard
- 1/8 teaspoon garlic powder
- 3/4 cup white rhineskellar wine
- 2 loaves crusty French bread

Direction

- About one hour before you want to serve the fondue mix all the ingredients, except the wine, in a saucepan.
- Stir and mix well on low heat until the cheeses have melted and everything is blended and heated thoroughly.
- Remove from heat and set aside.
- Cut the French bread into "two-bite" chunks.
- Right before serving, add the wine to the fondue, mix well and reheat on low until thoroughly warm.
- Place in a fondue pot or chafing dish, and serve with the chunks of French bread.

Nutrition Information

- Calories: 1442.1
- Sugar: 2.7
- Cholesterol: 213.5
- Total Fat: 73
- Saturated Fat: 43.4
- Sodium: 2206.6
- Fiber: 6.9
- Total Carbohydrate: 128.8
- Protein: 58.2

33. Warm And Creamy Swiss Cheese Dip With Caraway

Serving: 1 1/2 cups | Prep: 5mins | Ready in:

Ingredients

- 6 ounces swiss cheese, grated, or slices cut up
- 1 tablespoon flour
- 1/2 cup buttermilk
- 1/2 cup apple cider
- 1/2 teaspoon caraway seed

Direction

- In small bowl, toss cheese and flour.
- In small saucepan, heat buttermilk and cider.
- Add cheese and caraway seeds.
- Stir till melted.
- Keep warm while serving.
- Serve with chunks of rye bread for dipping.

Nutrition Information

- Calories: 484.9
- Total Fat: 32.4
- Fiber: 0.4
- Sugar: 5.4
- Total Carbohydrate: 14.3
- Saturated Fat: 20.6
- Sodium: 303.7
- Cholesterol: 107.6
- Protein: 33.9

Chapter 2: Swiss Side Dish Recipes

***

34. "gilded" Zucchini

Serving: 4-6 serving(s) | Prep: 10mins | Ready in:

Ingredients

- 2 lbs small tender zucchini
- salt, pepper to taste

- 2 eggs, well beaten
- 3 tablespoons milk
- 1/4 teaspoon salt
- breadcrumbs (coarse)
- oil or butter

Direction

- Wash and peel the zucchini and cut into long strips.
- Season with salt and pepper.
- Mix the eggs, milk and salt, dip the zucchini strips into the mixture and then roll in the breadcrumbs.
- Saute until crisp on the outside but not overcooked, about 2-3 minutes.
- Serve.

Nutrition Information

- Calories: 81.8
- Total Fat: 3.5
- Sodium: 204.7
- Cholesterol: 94.6
- Protein: 6.3
- Saturated Fat: 1.2
- Fiber: 2.3
- Sugar: 5.8
- Total Carbohydrate: 7.8

35. Alplermagrone (Swiss Gruyere Cheese Pasta)

Serving: 6-8 serving(s) | Prep: 15mins | Ready in:

Ingredients

- 17 ounces pasta (elbow macaroni)
- 3 tablespoons butter
- 1 dash vermouth (Gruppa is good also)
- 1 medium onion (thinly sliced)
- 1/2 lb bacon (swiss bacon know as lardoons)
- 1 cup whipping cream
- 8 ounces gruyere cheese (grated)
- salt freshly ground black pepper
- green onion (garnish-optional)

Direction

- Cook pasta per package directions; set aside.
- Cook bacon or lardon until cooked, but not crispy; set aside; pour off grease, but don't wipe out pan; add onions and butter, cook 3-5 minutes until onion is translucent, douse with vermouth or gruppa, steam a few minutes; add cream, bring just to hot heat, add cheese.
- Continue cooking until bubbly and creamy, add bacon, pour into bowls, serve with sliced green onions if desired.

Nutrition Information

- Calories: 824.2
- Total Fat: 50.9
- Fiber: 2.9
- Sugar: 3.1
- Total Carbohydrate: 63.5
- Saturated Fat: 25.8
- Sodium: 513.5
- Cholesterol: 137
- Protein: 27.3

36. Bacon Swiss Mac And Cheese

Serving: 6 serving(s) | Prep: 5mins | Ready in:

Ingredients

- 1 lb whole wheat penne
- 1/4 teaspoon garlic powder
- 1 1/2 cups low-fat buttermilk
- 1/4 cup chicken broth, low sodium
- 2 tablespoons whole wheat flour
- 1 1/2 cups low-fat swiss cheese
- 1/4 cup parmesan cheese
- 1/2 teaspoon dried thyme
- 1/2 teaspoon dried basil
- 2 slices turkey bacon, chopped

Direction

- 1. In a large pot boil salted water and cook pasta for 8 minutes then drain and set aside.
- 2. In a bowl mix the milk, broth and flour and whisk until flour is dissolved. Then pour the milk mixture, garlic powder, basil, thyme, and a pinch of salt and pepper into a sauce pan sprayed with cooking spray and cook over medium heat for 3-4 minutes or until milk begins to thicken. Then add the Swiss cheese, and parmesan cheese and continue to stir until cheese is melted (around 3 minutes).
- 3. In a small pan sprayed with cooking spray cook the bacon pieces over medium heat for 3-4 minutes or until crispy. Then set bacon aside on a plate lined with a paper towel.
- 4. Combine the pasta and cheese sauce and toss well. Then top with bacon pieces and serve.

Nutrition Information

- Calories: 388.6
- Total Fat: 5.5
- Saturated Fat: 2.6
- Total Carbohydrate: 63.4
- Cholesterol: 21.9
- Protein: 25.4
- Sodium: 308.6
- Fiber: 6.7
- Sugar: 3.6

37. Bacon And Swiss Scalloped Potatoes

Serving: 12 serving(s) | Prep: 45mins | Ready in:

Ingredients

- 3 tablespoons butter
- 2 lbs russet potatoes, peeled, sliced 1/8-inch thick
- 1 large yellow onion, thinly sliced
- 2 tablespoons chopped fresh parsley
- 2 slices bacon, cooked and chopped
- 2 1/2 cups grated swiss cheese
- 1/2 cup grated parmesan cheese
- 2 cups half-and-half
- salt and pepper

Direction

- Preheat oven to 350F and butter a 9x13 in casserole dish with 1 1/2 Tbsps. butter.
- Layer the bottom of the casserole dish with 1/3 of the potato slices. Sprinkle with salt and pepper. Layer on 1/2 of the sliced onions and 1/2 cup of the Swiss cheese. Layer on 1/2 of the bacon, 1/2 of the parsley. Sprinkle with a little of the Parmesan.
- Repeat by layering on 1/3 of the potato slices, sprinkle again with salt and pepper. Layer on the remaining sliced onions, 1/2 cup of the Swiss cheese, the remaining bacon, parsley and sprinkle with Parmesan.
- Top with the remaining potato slices. Add the half and half. Dot the potatoes with the remaining 1 1/2 Tbsps. of butter.
- Cover with aluminum foil and bake for one hour. Remove the foil and sprinkle on the remaining Swiss and Parmesan cheese. Return to the oven for an additional 40 minutes.
- When done, the potatoes should be tender and liquid mostly absorbed.

Nutrition Information

- Calories: 262.4
- Cholesterol: 49.5
- Fiber: 1.9
- Sugar: 1.5
- Total Carbohydrate: 17.7
- Total Fat: 16.8
- Saturated Fat: 10
- Sodium: 180.6
- Protein: 11

38. Bacon, Swiss Chard, Potato, And Vegetable Soul Satisfying Soup

Serving: 12 serving(s) | Prep: 20mins | Ready in:

Ingredients

- 8 ounces bacon, chopped
- 3 carrots, peeled and diced
- 3 celery ribs, diced
- 2 onions, diced
- 1 lb swiss chard (leaves julienned, fibery stalks diced)
- 2 bay leaves
- 3 potatoes, diced
- 6 garlic cloves, diced
- 1 gallon chicken stock (preferably your homemade, but purchased stock will work too)
- salt and black pepper

Direction

- I think it's easier to cut bacon when it's just out of the freezer. Anyway, cut the bacon across the strips, cutting it into small cross-sections of bacon strips. Add the bacon to a heavy-bottomed large soup pot over a medium flame. Render the bacon fat, stirring frequently to keep it from burning to the bottom of the pan. Once the bacon is crispy (but not burnt), remove it to a paper towel lined bowl/plate with a slotted spoon.
- Into the hot, delicious bacon fat add the carrots, celery, onion, Swiss chard stalks, and bay leaves. Sauté until vegetables soften, release liquid, and brown a bit (maybe up to 10 minutes or so?). The browning (but not burning) will develop additional flavour that will help to flavour your soup.
- Once the veggies have caramelized a bit, add the garlic, potatoes, and black pepper. Sauté a few minutes until garlic is fragrant but not burnt.
- Add the Swiss chard leaves, and stir well. The garlic and vegetable infused fat should evenly coat and cling to the contents on the pot. Add the chicken stock, enough to cover the veggies, cover the pot, and over a high flame bring to a boil, and reduce heat to simmer.
- Keep the soup at a bare simmer for 30 - 45 minutes or so, stirring occasionally, until vegetables are done to your liking. Taste and adjust the salt and black pepper. At this point, you can enjoy the soup as is, or you can use an immersion blender (or the tool of your choice) to further meld the flavours.
- Serve hot how you like it. With the crunchy bacon pieces, crusty bread, drizzled with a little olive oil, topped with a dollop of sour cream, dusted with a fresh turn of black pepper--the options are endless.

Nutrition Information

- Calories: 267.6
- Saturated Fat: 3.9
- Total Fat: 12.6
- Sodium: 718.1
- Fiber: 2.6
- Sugar: 7.6
- Total Carbohydrate: 26.2
- Cholesterol: 22.4
- Protein: 12.5

39. Berner Rösti

Serving: 6 serving(s) | Prep: 20mins | Ready in:

Ingredients

- 2 -2 1/2 lbs parboiled potatoes
- 1 teaspoon salt
- 1/2 teaspoon fresh minced rosemary
- 2 tablespoons melted butter
- 2 tablespoons lard or 2 tablespoons butter
- 4 slices bacon, diced
- 1 -2 tablespoon milk

Direction

- Peel the parboiled potatoes, grate into thin strips and mix with the salt.
- Heat the butter and lard (or all butter) in a nonstick frying pan. Add the diced bacon and potato and fry gently, stirring frequently.
- Bring together into a cake and cover with an upside-down plate. Fry over gentle heat for 20 minutes.
- Pour the milk over the top and fry, covered, for about another 10 minutes. Tip out onto the plate and serve.

Nutrition Information

- Calories: 215.1
- Total Fat: 10.7
- Saturated Fat: 5
- Fiber: 3.3
- Sugar: 1.2
- Cholesterol: 18.2
- Sodium: 476.1
- Total Carbohydrate: 26.6
- Protein: 3.8

40. Blitva (Croatian Swiss Chard Dish)

Serving: 4 serving(s) | Prep: 10mins | Ready in:

Ingredients

- 2 lbs swiss chard (preferably red)
- 3-4 medium potatoes
- 2-3 garlic cloves
- 2-3 tablespoons olive oil
- salt
- pepper

Direction

- Bring a large pot of salted water to a boil.
- Add peeled and cubed (1/2-1 in cubes) potatoes.
- Rinse the Swiss chard, remove tough stems, and cut into 1/2 in strips (or just tear into large pieces).
- When potatoes are almost done, add the Swiss chard, and cook all together for an additional 10 minutes (15 minutes if the chard is older).
- Sauté garlic on olive oil, and add the cooked drained chard and potatoes to it (you may keep some water so that it looks like a thick soup).
- Salt and pepper to taste.
- Stir and cook for 1 more minute in order to bring all flavours together.

Nutrition Information

- Calories: 228
- Saturated Fat: 1
- Fiber: 7.2
- Sugar: 3.8
- Total Carbohydrate: 36.9
- Total Fat: 7.4
- Sodium: 493.5
- Cholesterol: 0
- Protein: 7.4

41. Creamy Swiss Spinach Bake

Serving: 4 serving(s) | Prep: 25mins | Ready in:

Ingredients

- 2 (10 ounce) packages frozen chopped spinach, thawed and drained well
- 4 tablespoons butter
- 3 tablespoons flour
- 1 1/2 teaspoons Dijon mustard
- salt and pepper
- 1 cup half-and-half cream, divided
- 1/3 cup grated swiss cheese
- 4 tablespoons parmesan cheese

Direction

- Set oven to 350 degrees.
- Butter 1 2-qt casserole dish.
- In a medium saucepan, melt butter.
- Mix in flour to make a roux.
- Add mustard and cream, whisking until thickened; add Swiss cheese, 2 TBSP Parmesan cheese and 1 cup half and half cream; mix well.
- Remove from heat; cool 5 minutes.
- In a bowl, mix together spinach, the cooked cream sauce, salt and pepper to taste.
- Turn into prepared casserole dish.
- Top with remaining 2 TBSP Parmesan cheese.
- Bake for 20-25 minutes, or until hot and bubbly.

Nutrition Information

- Calories: 302.8
- Cholesterol: 65.6
- Protein: 12.5
- Total Fat: 23.6
- Saturated Fat: 14.5
- Sodium: 326.5
- Fiber: 4.6
- Sugar: 1.6
- Total Carbohydrate: 14.1

42. Fried Potato Cake

Serving: 4 serving(s) | Prep: 20mins | Ready in:

Ingredients

- 3 medium potatoes (1 lb)
- 1/4 cup onion, finely chopped
- 2 garlic cloves, minced
- 1/2 teaspoon salt
- 1/8 teaspoon pepper
- 2 tablespoons butter
- 1/2 cup cheese, shredded (The recipe calls for gruyere or emmentaler or swiss cheese, shredded, but I know the other two are h)

Direction

- Wash the potatoes.
- In a large covered saucepan, cook the whole potatoes in enough boiling salted water to cover for 20 to 25 minutes or until almost tender; drain.
- Chill several hours or overnight.
- Peel the potatoes; shred enough to make 3 cups.
- Combine the shredded potatoes, onion, garlic, salt, and pepper.
- In a 10-inch skillet, melt the butter.
- Using a spatula, pat the potato mixture into the skillet, leaving a 1/2 inch space around the edge.
- Cook potato mixture, uncovered, over low heat about 20 minutes or until the underside is crisp and golden brown.
- Use a spatula to loosen the potatoes from the skillet.
- Place a plate or baking sheet on top the skillet.
- Invert the skillet to remove the potatoes.
- If necessary, add more butter to the skillet.
- Slide the potato cake back into the skillet, browned side up; cook the unbrowned side for 5 minutes.
- Sprinkle the shredded cheese on top of the potato cake; cover, and cook 5 minutes more or until the potatoes are golden brown and the cheese is melted.
- Cut the potato cake into four wedges and serve.
- Garnish with sliced green onions, cut parsley, or sour cream if you wish.

Nutrition Information

- Calories: 227.1
- Saturated Fat: 5.9
- Sodium: 488.1
- Fiber: 3.7
- Sugar: 1.7
- Total Fat: 9.4
- Total Carbohydrate: 30.6
- Cholesterol: 24.3

- Protein: 6.3

43. Orecchiette With Swiss Chard, Tomatoes And Goat Cheese

Serving: 4 serving(s) | Prep: 10mins | Ready in:

Ingredients

- 3/4 lb orecchiette
- 1 bunch swiss chard, stems separated from leaves, each chopped
- 1 tablespoon extra virgin olive oil
- 1 lb tomatoes, cut in small dice
- 1 pinch red pepper flakes
- 2 garlic cloves, minced
- salt freshly ground black pepper
- 1 teaspoon fresh herbs of choice, chopped (basil or rosemary are particularly good here)
- 2 ounces goat cheese, crumbled (1/2 cup)

Direction

- Cook pasta according to package instructions. Reserve ½ cup pasta water prior to draining pasta.
- Meanwhile, heat 1 tablespoon of the olive oil over medium high heat in a large, heavy skillet, and add the chard stems and sauté for 2-3 minutes, then add tomatoes and the red pepper flakes. Cook, stirring often, until tender, 2-3 minutes. Add the garlic and salt to taste, and stir for 30 seconds. Then stir in the chopped chard leaves and the herbs. Stir together for a few seconds, then turn the heat to very low.
- Add about 1/2 cup of the pasta water to the pan with the chard mixture. Stir in the goat cheese. Drain the pasta, transfer to the pan and toss with the chard, tomatoes and goat cheese mixture. Season to taste with salt and pepper. Serve hot.

Nutrition Information

- Calories: 440
- Fiber: 5.7
- Protein: 17.1
- Total Fat: 9.3
- Sodium: 288.8
- Sugar: 6.7
- Total Carbohydrate: 72.8
- Cholesterol: 11.2
- Saturated Fat: 3.7

44. Rachael Ray's Savory Swiss Chard

Serving: 4 servings chard, 4 serving(s) | Prep: 10mins | Ready in:

Ingredients

- 2 tablespoons extra virgin olive oil (EVOO baby!!)
- 1 bunch swiss chard (any one, green, red or rainbow(stemmed and coarsely chopped)
- 1/4 teaspoon grated nutmeg
- 1/2 teaspoon smoked paprika or 1/2 teaspoon ground cumin
- salt, to your tastes
- pepper, to your tastes
- 1 teaspoon Worcestershire sauce
- 1/2 cup chicken stock

Direction

- In a large skillet, heat the EVOO over medium high heat. When the oil is hot, add the greens to the pan and wilt.
- Season the greens with nutmeg and smoked sweet paprika or the cumin.
- Salt and pepper and add the Worcestershire sauce.
- Add the chicken stock and simmer for a few minutes then serve!

Nutrition Information

- Calories: 91.3
- Sodium: 261.5
- Fiber: 1.7
- Sugar: 1.7
- Total Carbohydrate: 5.2
- Total Fat: 7.4
- Cholesterol: 0.9
- Protein: 2.5
- Saturated Fat: 1.1

45. Rosti With Mushrooms

Serving: 6-8 serving(s) | Prep: 4hours25mins | Ready in:

Ingredients

- 4 -6 potatoes, unpeeled
- 1/2 cup butter
- 1 onion, chopped
- 1 lb button mushrooms or 1 lb cremini mushroom, sliced
- 2 tablespoons fresh rosemary or 2 tablespoons thyme, chopped
- salt and pepper, to taste
- 2 tablespoons vegetable oil
- 2 tablespoons fresh parsley, finely chopped

Direction

- In saucepan, cover potatoes with cold water, bring to boil, reduce heat, cover and simmer until potatoes are tender yet still firm in center (about 15 minutes).
- Drain and cool; peel and refrigerate until chilled.
- Meanwhile, in skillet, melt 2 tbsp of the butter and cook onion mushrooms until lightly browned.
- Transfer to bowl; refrigerate until chilled.
- Grate potatoes into large bowl; add mushroom mixture, rosemary and salt pepper to taste.
- In 8-inch nonstick skillet, heat about 1 tbsp of remaining butter and 1 tbsp of the oil over medium-high heat; press half the potato mixture evenly over skillet.
- Reduce heat to medium; cook until underside is golden (5 to 7 minutes); invert onto plate.
- Heat about 1 tbsp butter in skillet; slide uncooked side of rosti into skillet; cook until golden (5 to 7 minutes).
- Repeat with remaining potato mixture.
- Garnish with parsley.

Nutrition Information

- Calories: 310.3
- Fiber: 4.3
- Sugar: 3.4
- Cholesterol: 40.7
- Protein: 5.6
- Total Fat: 20.3
- Saturated Fat: 10.4
- Sodium: 149
- Total Carbohydrate: 29.2

46. Sauerkraut Potatoes

Serving: 4 serving(s) | Prep: 5mins | Ready in:

Ingredients

- 500 g sauerkraut
- 1 onion, small, grated
- 1 granny smith apple, cored grated
- 1 tablespoon butter
- 4 potatoes, peel cut in quarters
- 1 cup water
- pepper

Direction

- Place the sauerkraut in a pan. Push the potatoes into the sauerkraut.
- Sprinkle over the onion and apple pepper and dot with butter. Add water.
- Bring to the boil and then turn down heat and simmer gently until potatoes are cooked, about 30-40 minutes. Check liquid level making sure it doesn't catch. Serve.

Nutrition Information

- Calories: 247.9
- Total Fat: 3.4
- Sugar: 9.8
- Sodium: 867.7
- Fiber: 9.9
- Total Carbohydrate: 51.4
- Cholesterol: 7.6
- Protein: 5.9
- Saturated Fat: 1.9

47. Sauteed Swiss Chard And Corn

Serving: 4 serving(s) | Prep: 5mins | Ready in:

Ingredients

- 8 slices maple bacon (Cooked Crisp Chopped)
- 2 cups fresh corn (2 ears corn, Kernels removed)
- 1/2 cup shallot (Chopped)
- 1 fresh garlic clove (Chopped)
- 2 lbs fresh swiss chard (Red Chard, Chopped)
- 1 tablespoon lemon thyme (Chopped)
- 1 teaspoon lemon zest
- 2 tablespoons fresh lemon juice
- 1 teaspoon fine sea salt
- 2 teaspoons fresh ground black pepper
- 3 lemons (Cut 2-lemons in wedges)

Direction

- In a large sauté pan cook bacon until crisp and remove all grease except for 2-tablespoons.
- Add bacon bits, corn, chopped shallots, chopped garlic and sauté until garlic is soft.
- Add Red Swiss Chard, fresh lemon thyme, lemon zest, salt and pepper. Sauté until chard starts to wilt, add fresh lemon juice and sauté for 1-2 minutes.
- Season with fine sea salt and fresh ground pepper to taste.

- Place the Red Swiss Chard on hot plates and serve.
- Garnish with fresh lemon wedges.

Nutrition Information

- Calories: 118.9
- Total Fat: 1.3
- Saturated Fat: 0.2
- Sodium: 818.2
- Fiber: 5.3
- Protein: 5.5
- Sugar: 4.9
- Total Carbohydrate: 27.5
- Cholesterol: 0

48. Sauteed Swiss Chard With Red Onions

Serving: 10 serving(s) | Prep: 10mins | Ready in:

Ingredients

- 3 lbs swiss chard, stems removed and reserved with leaves torn into bite-size pieces
- 2 tablespoons olive oil, divided
- 10 cloves garlic, peeled and halved
- 2 medium red onions, peeled and chopped
- salt and pepper

Direction

- Cut out the tough, triangular inner core of each leaf of Swiss chard and cut into 1/4- to 1/2-inch slices.
- Rinse the leaves and stems separately and reserve.
- In a large non-stick skillet, heat 1 tablespoon olive oil over medium heat.
- Add the garlic and cook until it turns golden brown; don't let the garlic get too brown or it will be bitter.
- Remove the garlic and set aside.
- Reserve the oil in the skillet.

- Add the remaining 1 tablespoon olive oil to the skillet and the onions.
- Sauté over medium heat until tender, about 5 minutes.
- Add the chopped stems from the Swiss chard and continue to cook over medium heat, stirring frequently, until the stems are very tender, 15 to 20 minutes.
- Add the Swiss chard leaves, season with salt and pepper and cover.
- Cook 10 minutes, stirring often; you may need to add 1/2 cup chicken stock or water to keep the leaves moist.
- Transfer to a serving bowl and top with the crispy garlic.

Nutrition Information

- Calories: 63
- Saturated Fat: 0.4
- Sodium: 291.6
- Sugar: 2.5
- Total Carbohydrate: 8.1
- Cholesterol: 0
- Protein: 2.9
- Total Fat: 3
- Fiber: 2.6

49. Simply Swiss Hash Browns #5FIX

Serving: 6 serving(s) | Prep: 10mins | Ready in:

Ingredients

- 1/2 medium onion, diced
- 1 (20 ounce) package Simply Potatoes® Shredded Hash Browns
- 1/2-1 cup shredded baby swiss cheese
- 1/3 cup chopped fresh parsley
- 3 tablespoons olive oil

Direction

- Saute diced onion over medium heat in 3 tablespoons Olive Oil until translucent.
- Add Simply Potatoes Shredded Hash Browns and lightly brown.
- Shred 1/2 to 1 cup Baby Swiss cheese and sprinkle over hash browns.
- Reduce heat to low and cover potatoes to allow Swiss Cheese to melt.
- Sprinkle fresh parsley over potatoes and serve.

Nutrition Information

- Calories: 106.3
- Sodium: 23.5
- Protein: 3.2
- Total Fat: 9.8
- Saturated Fat: 2.9
- Fiber: 0.3
- Sugar: 0.6
- Total Carbohydrate: 1.7
- Cholesterol: 10.1

50. Spicy Swiss Chard With Lemon

Serving: 6 serving(s) | Prep: 2mins | Ready in:

Ingredients

- 1 tablespoon olive oil
- 16 cups swiss chard
- 1/2 teaspoon crushed red pepper flakes
- 3 garlic cloves, minced
- 1 tablespoon lemon juice
- 1/8 teaspoon salt

Direction

- Heat oil in a large Dutch oven over medium heat.
- Add chard, sauté until lightly wilted, 1 to 2 minute.
- Stir in pepper and garlic.
- Cover and cook 4 min or until tender, stirring occasionally.

- Uncover and cook 3 minutes or until liquid evaporates.
- Stir in juice and salt.

Nutrition Information

- Calories: 41.2
- Protein: 1.8
- Total Fat: 2.5
- Sodium: 253.3
- Fiber: 1.6
- Total Carbohydrate: 4.3
- Cholesterol: 0
- Saturated Fat: 0.3
- Sugar: 1.2

51. Sweet And Sour Cabbage

Serving: 4 serving(s) | Prep: 10mins | Ready in:

Ingredients

- 1 small cabbage
- butter or margarine
- 1/2 lb leftover ham or 1/2 lb fried bacon
- 1 medium onion
- 2 tablespoons vinegar
- salt and pepper
- 1/2 cup sugar

Direction

- Boil cabbage in salt water until soft, drain and put into a frying pan with some butter.
- Add the cut up ham or fried bacon.
- Add onion, vinegar, salt, pepper and sugar.
- Simmer 1/2 hour.
- I added 3 slices of bacon and the rest ham.

Nutrition Information

- Calories: 235.8
- Protein: 15.5
- Total Fat: 3.5
- Fiber: 4.5
- Sugar: 32.5
- Cholesterol: 29.5
- Saturated Fat: 1.1
- Sodium: 892.7
- Total Carbohydrate: 37.8

52. Swiss Beef Crescent Ring

Serving: 4 serving(s) | Prep: 30mins | Ready in:

Ingredients

- 3 tablespoons sweet white onions, finely chopped
- 1 teaspoon lemon juice
- 1 1/2 cups swiss cheese, shredded
- 1/2 cup sweet red pepper, finely chopped
- 1/4 cup yellow sweet pepper, finely chopped
- 1/2 cup wild mushroom, finely chopped
- 1 1/2 cups beef, leftovers, diced
- 1 (8 ounce) package Pillsbury Refrigerated Crescent Dinner Rolls
- 2 tablespoons dry mustard
- 2 tablespoons fresh parsley, finely chopped
- 1 teaspoon salt
- 1/2 teaspoon black pepper, fresh ground
- 1 tablespoon margarine, softened

Direction

- Preheat oven to 350°F.
- In a large bowl mix the onion, mustard, parsley, salt, pepper, margarine and lemon juice together and blend well.
- Add the cheese, colored peppers, mushrooms and the diced beef, mix lightly.
- Separate the dough into 8 triangles and place on a greased cookie sheet.
- Arrange the triangles in a circle with the bases over lapping.
- The center opening should be about 3 inches in diameter.
- Points should be towards the outside.

- Spoon the filling in a ring over bases of triangle.
- Fold the points of the triangle over the filling and tuck under the base at the center of the circle.
- When finished it should look like a round ring.
- Bake in a preheated oven for 30 minutes.
- Remove from oven and allow to cool 5 - 10 minutes before serving.
- Perfect served with a fresh salad.

Nutrition Information

- Calories: 957.1
- Cholesterol: 149.8
- Protein: 24.9
- Total Fat: 79.1
- Sodium: 980.4
- Sugar: 4.5
- Saturated Fat: 33.7
- Fiber: 3.3
- Total Carbohydrate: 36

53. Swiss Chard With Chickpeas And Feta

Serving: 4-6 serving(s) | Prep: 10mins | Ready in:

Ingredients

- 1/4 cup extra virgin olive oil
- 3 lbs swiss chard, stemmed and leaves rinsed but not dried
- 4 scallions, white and light green parts only, thinly sliced
- 1/4 cup chopped dill
- 2 garlic cloves, minced
- 1 (19 ounce) can chickpeas, drained and rinsed
- salt freshly ground black pepper
- 3 ounces feta cheese, crumbled

Direction

- Preheat the oven to 400°. Coat an 8-inch-square nonreactive baking dish with 1 tablespoon of the olive oil.
- Put the chard in a large pot, cover and cook over high heat, stirring occasionally, until wilted, about 4 minutes. Drain and rinse under cold water; squeeze dry and coarsely chop.
- In a medium bowl, toss the chard with the remaining 3 tablespoons of olive oil, scallions, dill, garlic and chickpeas. Season with salt and pepper.
- Spoon the mixture into the prepared baking dish. Sprinkle the feta on top and push the cheese into the greens. Bake for 15 to 20 minutes, until sizzling hot. Serve immediately.

Nutrition Information

- Calories: 411.1
- Total Fat: 20.6
- Fiber: 11.8
- Sugar: 5
- Saturated Fat: 5.5
- Sodium: 1382.7
- Total Carbohydrate: 45.8
- Cholesterol: 20.1
- Protein: 16.4

54. Swiss Chard With Raisins And Pine Nuts

Serving: 4 serving(s) | Prep: 25mins | Ready in:

Ingredients

- 1 1/2 lbs swiss chard (preferably rainbow or red)
- 1/2 cup pine nuts
- 3 tablespoons olive oil
- 1 medium onion, finely chopped
- 1/4 cup golden raisin, chopped
- 1 cup water

Direction

- Tear chard leaves from stems, then coarsely chopped stem and leaves separately.
- Toast pine nuts in a heavy pot over moderate heat, stirring constantly until golden, about 1.5 to 2 minutes.
- Sauté onion in oil for about 1 minute, then add chard stems and cook, stirring occasionally for 2 minute.
- Add raisins and 1/2 cup of water and simmer, covered, until stems are softened, about 3 minutes.
- Add chard leaves and remaining 1/2 cup of water and simmer, partially covered until leaves are tender, about 3 minutes. Serve immediately.

Nutrition Information

- Calories: 274.3
- Total Fat: 22.1
- Saturated Fat: 2.3
- Sodium: 366.3
- Sugar: 9
- Protein: 5.9
- Fiber: 4.1
- Total Carbohydrate: 18.6
- Cholesterol: 0

55. Swiss Chard In Sauce Gruyere

Serving: 8 serving(s) | Prep: 30mins | Ready in:

Ingredients

- 2 bunches swiss chard
- 3 tablespoons flour
- 2 1/2 tablespoons butter
- 2 cups chicken stock
- 1 1/2 cups gruyere cheese, grated
- 2 tablespoons oil
- 1 dash Old Bay Seasoning
- 1/4 teaspoon nutmeg
- black pepper, to taste
- 1 pinch salt

Direction

- Separate the stems and leaves of the chard.
- Wash the stems and cut diagonally into 1-inch pieces.
- Wash the leaves in 2 changes of water as they can be sandy.
- Spin dry and coarsely chop the leaves.
- Heat the oil in a wok or large pan.
- Add the stem pieces and a pinch of salt and stir-fry until tender, about 5 minutes.
- Add the leaves and cover.
- Steam until leaves wilt, stirring occasionally.
- If mixture is too wet, uncover and cook off excess liquid.
- Transfer to an oven proof casserole and set aside.
- Preheat oven to 350°F.
- Prepare a Sauce Velouté.
- Melt butter in a saucepan.
- Add flour and cook, stirring for 3-4 minutes.
- Add 1/4 cup stock, stirring to form a paste.
- Continue adding stock, a little at a time, stirring to incorporate before adding more stock.
- This will prevent lumping.
- When all the stock has been added, season with a dash of Old Bay and a grinding of pepper.
- Continue to cook, stirring, until the sauce is thick enough to coat the spoon.
- Remove from heat, stir in nutmeg, whisk in cheese, pour over chard.
- Finish in oven 20-25 minutes.

Nutrition Information

- Calories: 196.4
- Sodium: 403.3
- Fiber: 1.6
- Sugar: 2.1
- Total Carbohydrate: 8.1
- Cholesterol: 33.6
- Protein: 9.6
- Total Fat: 14.5
- Saturated Fat: 6.8

56. Swiss Chard, Potato, And Chickpea Stew

Serving: 4-6 serving(s) | Prep: 15mins | Ready in:

Ingredients

- 1 lb swiss chard, tough stems removed, leaves washed well and chopped
- 3 tablespoons olive oil
- 1 1/2 lbs baking potatoes, peeled and sliced 3/4-inch thick (about 3)
- 1 onion, chopped
- 2 garlic cloves, minced
- 1 teaspoon paprika
- 1/4 teaspoon turmeric
- 1/8 teaspoon cayenne pepper
- 1 teaspoon salt
- 2 cups chickpeas, drained and rinsed (one 19-ounce can)
- 3 cups low sodium chicken broth
- 1 cup water
- 2 hard-boiled eggs, cut into wedges

Direction

- Bring a medium pot of salted water to a boil. Add the chard and cook for 3 minutes. Drain thoroughly and set aside.
- In a Dutch oven, heat the oil over moderate heat. Add the potatoes and onion and sauté, stirring frequently, until the potatoes start to brown, about 5 minutes. Add the garlic, paprika, turmeric, cayenne, and salt and cook, stirring, until fragrant, about 1 minute.
- Add the cooked chard, chickpeas, broth, and water. Bring to a simmer and cook until the potatoes are tender, about 15 minutes. Serve the stew garnished with the hard-cooked eggs.

Nutrition Information

- Calories: 485.1
- Saturated Fat: 2.8
- Sodium: 1277.5
- Cholesterol: 93.2
- Protein: 18.4
- Total Fat: 15.8
- Sugar: 4.5
- Total Carbohydrate: 71.6
- Fiber: 10.9

57. Tomatoes Fribourg Style (Tomates Fribourgeoises)

Serving: 4 serving(s) | Prep: 15mins | Ready in:

Ingredients

- 2 large tomatoes
- 2 tablespoons brown sugar
- 3/4 cup gruyere or 3/4 cup swiss cheese, finely grated
- 2 cups mashed potatoes (prepared, instant or leftovers)
- 1 green onion, chopped
- 1 dash white pepper
- butter or margarine

Direction

- Preheat oven to 350°F.
- Wash and halve tomatoes.
- Scoop out most of the flesh and discard liquid and seeds.
- Sprinkle each tomato half with 1/2 tablespoon brown sugar.
- Mix 1/2 cup grated cheese with mashed potatoes, white parts of green onion, and pepper.
- Stuff each tomato with equal amounts.
- Dot each with a little butter.
- Place into a well-greased, shallow baking dish and bake for 10 minutes.
- Remove, sprinkle with remaining cheese, and bake for another 5 minutes.

- Remove, sprinkle with remaining green onion and serve.

Nutrition Information

- Calories: 214.7
- Total Fat: 7.3
- Saturated Fat: 4.2
- Total Carbohydrate: 29.1
- Sodium: 392.2
- Fiber: 2.8
- Sugar: 10.8
- Cholesterol: 24.4
- Protein: 8.9

58. Zwiebelwähe (Swiss Onion Tart)

Serving: 8-10 serving(s) | Prep: 2hours | Ready in:

Ingredients

- Crust
- 1 1/2 cups flour
- 1/2 teaspoon baking powder
- 1/4 teaspoon kosher salt
- 8 tablespoons unsalted butter, chilled and cubed
- 1/4 cup ice-cold water
- Filling
- 3 ounces bacon, finely chopped (known as Speck in Switzerland)
- 3 tablespoons unsalted butter
- 1 1/2 lbs white onions, finely chopped (about 3)
- kosher salt, to taste
- 1/2 cup milk
- 1/2 cup heavy cream
- 3 eggs
- 3 ounces grated gruyere cheese or 3 ounces good quality swiss cheese
- fresh ground black pepper
- freshly grated nutmeg

Direction

- Crust:
- Pulse flour, baking powder, and salt in a food processor to combine. Add butter and pulse until pea-sized pieces form. Add water; pulse briefly. Transfer dough to a floured work surface; form into a disk. Wrap in plastic wrap; chill for 1 hour.
- Heat oven to 425°F. Transfer dough to a floured work surface. Roll dough into a 13-inch circle; transfer to an 11-inch fluted tart pan with a removable bottom, pressing into bottom and sides. Trim excess dough; chill for 30 minutes. Prick bottom of dough with a fork; cover bottom with a sheet of parchment paper; fill with pie weights or dried beans. Bake until crust is set, about 20 minutes. Remove paper and beans; bake until crust is light brown, about 15 minutes. Let cool.
- Filling:
- Cook bacon in a 4-quart saucepan over medium heat until crisp, 7-8 minutes. Using a slotted spoon, transfer bacon to a plate. Discard bacon fat; add butter. Add onions and season with salt; reduce heat to low, cover, and cook, stirring occasionally, until soft, about 10 minutes. Uncover; cook until lightly browned, 10 minutes. Let cool.
- Whisk milk, cream, and eggs in a bowl; add reserved bacon and onions along with cheese. Season with salt, pepper, and nutmeg. Pour filling into tart; place on baking sheet.
- Place tart in oven and reduce heat to 400°F. Bake until filling is golden brown and set, 45-50 minutes. Transfer tart to a wire rack to let cool completely before slicing and serving.

Nutrition Information

- Calories: 440.1
- Total Fat: 32.2
- Sodium: 247.5
- Fiber: 2.1
- Sugar: 3.8
- Total Carbohydrate: 27.3

- Saturated Fat: 18.1
- Cholesterol: 153.2
- Protein: 11.1

Chapter 3: Swiss Dessert Recipes

***

59. Baker's Fabulously Flawless Fudge

Serving: 4 dozen, 48 serving(s) | Prep: 25mins | Ready in:

Ingredients

- 1 1/2 cups pecans or 1 1/2 cups walnuts, chopped
- 16 (1 ounce) squares BAKER'S Semi-Sweet Chocolate (2 pkgs)
- 1 (300 ml) can sweetened condensed milk
- 2 teaspoons vanilla

Direction

- Spread nuts on cookie sheet and bake at 350°F (180°C) for 10 minutes to toast; cool.
- Melt chocolate with milk in large microwaveable bowl in microwave on HIGH 2 to 3 minutes or until chocolate is almost melted. Stir until chocolate is completely melted.
- Stir in vanilla and nuts. Spread in foil-lined 8 inch (20 cm) square pan.
- Chill 2 hours or until firm. Cut into squares.
- VARIATIONS: PEANUT BUTTER FUDGE - Omit nuts. Drop 1/2 cup (125 mL) peanut butter by teaspoonfuls on top of fudge. Swirl with knife to marble.
- WHITE CHOCOLATE LAYERED FUDGE - Prepare fudge as directed using 3/4 cup (175 mL) nuts, 1 pkg (225 g) Baker's Semi-Sweet Chocolate, 3/4 cup (175 mL) sweetened condensed milk and 1 tsp (5 mL) vanilla. Spread in prepared pan. Melt 1 pkg (170 g) Baker's White Chocolate. Stir in remaining 1/2 cup (125 mL) sweetened condensed milk. Spread over dark chocolate layer. Chill as directed.

Nutrition Information

- Calories: 93.9
- Saturated Fat: 2.3
- Total Carbohydrate: 10.6
- Sodium: 10.8
- Fiber: 0.9
- Sugar: 9.5
- Cholesterol: 2.6
- Protein: 1.3
- Total Fat: 6

60. Baseler Leckerli (Swiss Spice Cookies)

Serving: 60-72 cookies | Prep: 40mins | Ready in:

Ingredients

- 4 1/2 cups flour
- 1 tablespoon cinnamon
- 1 1/2 teaspoons ground cloves
- 1 teaspoon ground cardamom
- 1/2 teaspoon nutmeg
- 1 teaspoon baking soda
- 1 cup honey
- 1/2 cup sugar
- 2 tablespoons water
- 1/2 cup unblanched slivered almonds
- 1/2 cup candied orange peel, chopped
- 1/2 lemon, zest of, grated

Direction

- Preheat the oven to 350°F.
- Line 2 baking sheets with parchment.
- Sift together the flour, cinnamon, cloves, cardamom, nutmeg and baking soda.
- Combine honey, sugar and water in a small saucepan.
- Place over low heat until the honey just melts- do not let it boil.
- Transfer the mixture to the bowl of a heavy-duty mixer fitted with the dough hook.
- Let cool slightly.
- Add the sifted flour mixture, the almonds, orange peel and lemon zest.
- Blend until the mixture comes together in a heavy, sticky dough, adding a spoonful or two of water if needed.
- (The mixing can be done by hand, but it's labor intensive) Resist the urge to add more water to make the dough easier to handle; it would impair the texture of the finished cookies.
- Spread the dough about 1/2 to 1 inch thick on the baking sheets, forming 3 rectangles, each about 8 x 9 inches.
- Bake for about 20 minutes, until the tops turn a medium brown.
- When the dough rectangles have baked, remove pans to a rack and immediately brush the tops with glaze.
- Let cool for 10 minutes.
- Cut into 1 x 3-inch bars or into diamond shapes.
- Transfer to racks to cool completely.
- Ice with a simple sugar glaze.
- Store in airtight containers, placing wax paper between layers.
- Let rest at least 1 week, preferably longer.

Nutrition Information

- Calories: 63.6
- Saturated Fat: 0.1
- Fiber: 0.5
- Sugar: 6.4
- Protein: 1.2
- Total Fat: 0.6
- Sodium: 21.6
- Total Carbohydrate: 13.8
- Cholesterol: 0

61. Basler Lackerli (Swiss Spiced Honey Cookies)

Serving: 42 cookies | Prep: 45mins | Ready in:

Ingredients

- 3 cups all-purpose flour
- 2 teaspoons cinnamon
- 1/2 teaspoon ground cloves
- 1/2 teaspoon nutmeg, freshly grated
- 1 teaspoon baking powder
- 1/2 teaspoon baking soda
- 1 cup honey
- 1 cup granulated sugar
- 2 tablespoons kirsch
- 1/2 cup candied orange peel, finely chopped (about 3 oz)
- 1 1/2 cups almonds, whole natural (about 8 oz)
- 1 tablespoon water
- 1/4 cup granulated sugar
- 1 tablespoon confectioners' sugar

Direction

- Preheat oven to 325 degrees. Line bottom and sides of a buttered jelly-roll pan, 10 1/2 x 15 1/2 x 1-inch, with foil and butter foil.
- Make dough:
- Chop almonds very fine but not ground, preferably in a food processor. In a bowl whisk together flour, spices, baking powder, and baking soda. In a large heavy saucepan heat honey and granulated sugar over moderately low heat, stirring, just until sugar is dissolved. Remove pan from heat and stir in kirsch, orange peel, and almonds. Stir in flour mixture and cool dough 5 minutes.
- With floured hands, press dough evenly into pan. Put dough in oven and immediately reduce temperature to 300 degrees F. Bake

dough 25 - 30 mins, or until firm but not dry and hard, and cool in pan on a rack. Invert baked dough onto a cutting board. Discard foil and invert baked dough.
- Make glaze:
- Ina small saucepan heat water with granulated sugar over moderately low heat, stirring, just until sugar is dissolved. Sift in confectioners' sugar and stir until combined well.
- Pour hot glaze on baked dough and brush evenly over dough, brushing continuously until glaze crystallizes and whitens. Let glazed dough stand 10 minutes Trim off and discard edges of dough and cut into 2 x 1 1/2-inch rectangles. Keep cookies in an airtight container up to 2 weeks.

Nutrition Information

- Calories: 110.7
- Total Carbohydrate: 20.8
- Cholesterol: 0
- Protein: 2
- Total Fat: 2.7
- Saturated Fat: 0.2
- Sodium: 41
- Fiber: 0.9
- Sugar: 13

62. Candy Cane Brunch Cakes

Serving: 3 canes | Prep: 1hours | Ready in:

Ingredients

- 2 cups sour cream
- 1/2 cup warm water
- 1/3 cup sugar
- 2 eggs
- 2 packages dry yeast
- 1/4 cup softened butter
- 2 teaspoons salt
- 6 cups flour
- 1 can pie filling
- Icing
- 3 cups powdered sugar
- 3 tablespoons hot water
- 3 drops almond extract

Direction

- Heat sour cream over low heat until lukewarm.
- Put yeast in warm water.
- Add to sour cream.
- Add butter, sugar, salt, eggs, and 2 cups flour.
- Mix until smooth.
- Add remaining flour, enough so dough is easy to handle.
- Knead until smooth, about 10 min.
- Place in greased bowl, cover, let rise until double.
- Punch down and divide into 3 parts.
- Roll each into rectangle 15"x6".
- Place on greased baking sheet.
- Make 2" cuts at 1/2" intervals on both long sides of rectangle.
- Divide filling into 3 parts and spread onto dough.
- Criss-cross strips over filling and stretch dough to form curve of cane.
- Bake 15 to 20 mins at 375.
- Drizzle with icing.

Nutrition Information

- Calories: 1990.2
- Cholesterol: 249.1
- Protein: 36.8
- Sugar: 140.9
- Total Carbohydrate: 341.1
- Fiber: 7.7
- Total Fat: 53.6
- Saturated Fat: 31.2
- Sodium: 1796.9

63. Chocolate Almond Crisps

Serving: 40 cookies | Prep: 50mins | Ready in:

Ingredients

- 2 cups ground blanched almonds
- 1 1/2 cups icing sugar
- 4 tablespoons cocoa powder
- 2 1/2 teaspoons ground cinnamon
- 1/8 teaspoon ground cloves
- 3 ounces unsweetened chocolate
- 1/2 teaspoon almond extract
- 2 large egg whites

Direction

- Preheat the oven to 325°F.
- Line a couple of cookie trays with parchment paper.
- In a food processor, process the almonds with the sugar until finely ground.
- Add the cocoa, spices and broken up chocolate and process again, until the chocolate is finely ground.
- Process in the egg whites and the extract until it blends and forms a mass.
- Remove the dough, let sit for about 5 minutes.
- Roll out on a board sprinkled with icing sugar.
- Cut with cookie cutters and place on the trays.
- Bake in the centre of the oven for 10 to 12 minutes until almost firm and slightly puffed; they should not be browned.
- Let cool then peel from the paper.

Nutrition Information

- Calories: 73.6
- Fiber: 1.3
- Sugar: 4.8
- Cholesterol: 0
- Saturated Fat: 1
- Sodium: 4.9
- Total Fat: 5
- Total Carbohydrate: 6.9
- Protein: 2.1

64. Chocolate Pecan Toffee

Serving: 10 serving(s) | Prep: 30mins | Ready in:

Ingredients

- 1 cup butter
- 1 cup sugar
- 1 tablespoon corn syrup
- 3 tablespoons water
- 1/2 cup coarsely chopped pecans
- 1/4 cup finely chopped pecans
- 3/4 cup chocolate chips

Direction

- Butter sides of heavy saucepan.
- Cook the butter, sugar, corn syrup, and water over medium heat until it reaches 290 degrees, stirring constantly.
- Remove from heat.
- Spread coarsely chopped nuts evenly on a 9x9" baking pan.
- Pour sugar mixture onto baking pan.
- Spread to edges with a wooden spoon.
- Place finely chopped nuts on sugar mixture.
- Place chocolate chips on top of sugar mixture, then wait for them to melt.
- Once the chocolate chips melt, spread them evenly around sugar mixture and nuts.
- Put in cool place to harden.
- Break into pieces, and store covered in a refrigerator.

Nutrition Information

- Calories: 362.3
- Fiber: 1.5
- Total Carbohydrate: 30.5
- Cholesterol: 48.8
- Protein: 1.5
- Total Fat: 28.1
- Saturated Fat: 14.4
- Sodium: 132.3
- Sugar: 27.7

65. Date And Muesli Slice

Serving: 12-16 slices, 12-16 serving(s) | Prep: 10mins | Ready in:

Ingredients

- 3 1/2 cups light brown sugar
- 1 cup dried dates, chopped
- 1 cup self-rising flour
- 1/2 cup muesli (granola)
- 2 tablespoons roasted sunflower seeds
- 1 teaspoon poppy seed
- 2 tablespoons sultanas (golden raisins)
- 2/3 cup natural low-fat yogurt (plain)
- 1 egg, beaten
- 1 3/4 cups icing sugar, sifted (confectioner's sugar)
- lemon juice
- 1-2 tablespoon toasted pumpkin seeds

Direction

- Preheat the oven to 350F/180C/Gas4. Line an 11x17 shallow baking pan with baking parchment.
- Mix together all the ingredients except the icing sugar, lemon juice and pumpkin seeds.
- Spread the mixture evenly in the pan and bake for about 25 minutes, until golden brown. Remove from oven and allow to cool.
- To make the topping, put the icing sugar in a bowl and stir in just enough lemon juice to give a thick, spreading consistency.
- Spread the lemon topping over the baked mixture and sprinkle generously with pumpkin seeds.
- Allow icing to set before cutting into squares or bars.

Nutrition Information

- Calories: 427.8
- Protein: 3.5
- Saturated Fat: 0.5
- Sodium: 174.8
- Fiber: 1.8
- Sugar: 90.3
- Total Carbohydrate: 102.9
- Total Fat: 2
- Cholesterol: 16.3

66. Dutch Baby With Strawberries

Serving: 1 pancake, 2 serving(s) | Prep: 5mins | Ready in:

Ingredients

- For the batter
- 1 large egg, room temperature
- 1 1/2 ounces cake flour
- 1 1/2 ounces whole milk
- 1 tablespoon unsalted butter
- 1 tablespoon granulated sugar
- 1/2 teaspoon vanilla essence
- For the fruit
- 1 tablespoon granulated sugar
- 1 teaspoon vanilla essence
- 4 ounces fresh strawberries, sliced

Direction

- Preheat the oven to 400 F (200°C).
- Place sliced strawberries in a small bowl. Sprinkle with 1 tbsp. sugar and 1 tsp vanilla essence. Stir gently.
- In a large bowl, combine scrambled egg, flour, milk, sugar and vanilla essence. Mix well until mixture is smooth. Leave aside.
- Heat 6-inch iron skillet over medium-high heat. Place butter in the skillet and melt it. Be sure not to burn butter.
- Remove the skillet from the heat, place it to the kitchen board and immediately pour the batter in the skillet. In this point, do not mix the batter once you pour it to the skillet. Just pour all batter in the middle of the skillet.

- When done, carefully place the skillet immediately to the preheated oven.
- Bake for 10 mins being sure not to burn the sides. Remove from the oven, prick the dough with fork in the middle (not the sides) and return to the oven for more 5 minutes.
- When done, arrange fresh strawberries to the top and serve for breakfast while it is still warm.

Nutrition Information

- Calories: 258.3
- Sodium: 47.4
- Total Carbohydrate: 36.3
- Cholesterol: 110.5
- Saturated Fat: 4.9
- Sugar: 17.1
- Protein: 6.1
- Total Fat: 9.2
- Fiber: 1.5

67. Frittata Of Sweet Potatoes, Swiss Chard, Peppers And Onions

Serving: 6 serving(s) | Prep: 40mins | Ready in:

Ingredients

- 1 yellow pepper, roasted and thinly sliced
- 2 lbs sweet potatoes, about 3
- 5 eggs, use whole egg
- 5 egg whites
- salt, to taste
- black pepper, to taste
- 2 tablespoons olive oil
- 1 large Spanish onion, sliced with the grain
- 1 bunch swiss chard, about 6 oz., Prep as suggested before blanching
- 1 tablespoon parsley, chopped

Direction

- Preheat oven to 350 degrees F.
- Char the peppers on an open fire or under the broiler. Steam them for five minutes in a bag or covered bowl, and peel. Seed them, then cut into 1/4-inch strips.
- Prepare Swiss chard: Both the leaves and the stems of Swiss chard are edible. When preparing the chard for this recipe, remove the stems from the leaves. Slice the stems into ¼-inch pieces and blanch separately from the leaves. The leaves may be cut into spoon-size pieces.
- Bake potatoes in the oven until they are tender, 20 to 30 minutes. Allow them to cool at room temperature. When the potatoes have cooled, peel them and cut into 1/4-inch slices.
- Beat eggs and egg whites and season with salt and black pepper.
- Heat half the oil in a large, 10-inch sauté pan. Add the onions and sauté until brown. Season onions with salt and pepper and allow them to cool.
- Return sauté pan to stove on medium heat, and add the remaining olive oil. Add a layer of potatoes, followed by 1/3 of the onions, peppers, prepared Swiss chard and parsley.
- Pour a third of the egg mixture over the vegetables. Repeat until all of the ingredients are in the pan. You may need to push the layers of the frittata down gently so that all of the ingredients are covered by the egg mixture.
- Place the pan in a 350°F oven for 20 to 25 minutes or until the eggs are all set and the top is golden brown.
- Slide onto a warm serving platter and let cool for five minutes. Slice and serve.
- Prep includes prep and stove top time. Cooking time is baking time.

Nutrition Information

- Calories: 274.6
- Cholesterol: 155
- Protein: 12.4
- Saturated Fat: 2

- Sodium: 326.4
- Sugar: 8.4
- Total Carbohydrate: 37.7
- Total Fat: 8.8
- Fiber: 6.3

68. Frozen Swiss Roll Ice Cream Cake

Serving: 20-25 serving(s) | Prep: 20mins | Ready in:

Ingredients

- 2 (400 g) packages chocolate swiss rolls, individually wrapped, sliced in 4 (6 mini rolls in each package)
- 8 cups vanilla ice cream, softened
- 1/2 cup smucker's sundae syrup, Caramel Syrup, divided
- 1/2 cup smucker's sundae syrup, Chocolate Syrup, for garnish (optional)

Direction

- Line a 12 cup metal bowl with plastic wrap.
- Line inside of bowl with sliced Swiss rolls, allowing them to overlap if necessary. Reserve the remaining slices for the top.
- Fill with 2 cups of softened ice cream, spreading ice cream slightly up the sides of the bowl.
- Cover with 1/4 of the caramel syrup.
- Continue layering ice cream and alternating syrups, ending with ice cream.
- Place remaining Swiss roll slices on top.
- Cover with plastic wrap and freeze until firm, about 3 hours. To serve, invert onto serving dish, remove plastic wrap and garnish with additional sundae syrups.

Nutrition Information

- Calories: 134.2
- Total Fat: 6.3

- Cholesterol: 25.3
- Protein: 2
- Saturated Fat: 3.9
- Sodium: 52.5
- Fiber: 0.5
- Sugar: 14.8
- Total Carbohydrate: 18.4

69. Frozen Swiss Strawberries

Serving: 10-12 serving(s) | Prep: 10mins | Ready in:

Ingredients

- 1 lb brown sugar
- 4 lbs fresh strawberries

Direction

- Mix sugar and strawberries.
- Let stand for 10 minutes.
- Put in cartons and freeze.

Nutrition Information

- Calories: 230.6
- Saturated Fat: 0
- Sodium: 14.5
- Fiber: 3.6
- Sugar: 52.9
- Total Carbohydrate: 58.5
- Cholesterol: 0
- Total Fat: 0.5
- Protein: 1.3

70. Geneva Pear Flan

Serving: 8 serving(s) | Prep: 10mins | Ready in:

Ingredients

- 300 g shortcrust pastry

- 20 g flour
- 30 g sugar
- cinnamon, ground
- 8 pears, ripe, peeled, grated coarsely
- 50 g lemon peel, candied cut in small dice cut in small dice
- 50 g orange peel, candied, cut in small dice cut in small dice
- 100 g raisins
- 2 tablespoons white wine
- 1 tablespoon walnut oil
- 40 g brown sugar
- 100 ml cream

Direction

- Line a 24 cm wide flan ring with the pastry and prick well with a fork.
- Mix the sugar, cinnamon and flour thoroughly and sprinkle this onto the pastry base.
- Mix the pear slices, lemon and orange peel, raisins and oil together then spread this on to the pastry case. Moisten the mixture with the white wine (all or part of the wine, depending on the amount of pear juice in the flan ring).
- Sprinkle with the brown sugar and cover with cream.
- Bake for 30-35 minutes at 220°C
- Loosen the sides of the flan and leave to cool; turn out when cold. Serve cold.

Nutrition Information

- Calories: 453.5
- Total Fat: 17.6
- Saturated Fat: 5.5
- Fiber: 10.3
- Sodium: 191
- Sugar: 38.9
- Total Carbohydrate: 74.9
- Cholesterol: 14.2
- Protein: 4.1

71. Getränkter Zitronencake (Swiss Lemon Loaf)

Serving: 1 loaf | Prep: 25mins | Ready in:

Ingredients

- 250 g butter (8 7/8 ounces, at room temperature) or 250 g margarine (8 7/8 ounces, at room temperature)
- 250 g sugar (8 7/8 ounces)
- 5 eggs, at room temperature
- 2 lemons, zest of, only
- 250 g flour (8 7/8 ounces)
- 2 teaspoons baking powder
- 1 pinch salt
- Glaze
- 3 -4 lemons, juice of (100ml lemon juice or slightly more)
- 100 g icing sugar (3 1/2 ounces)

Direction

- The loaf pans in Switzerland are 9-10cm in width and adaptable in length. For this recipe you need to adapt the length to 28-30cm. However, I assume that this recipe will work equally well in a slightly different size of loaf pan.
- Beat the butter.
- Add some of the sugar, then an egg. Mix until well incorporated. Carry on with the remaining sugar and eggs the same way. Always make sure that the ingredients are well incorporated.
- Add the zest of the two lemons.
- Mix flour, baking powder and salt in a separate bowl. Then mix into the other ingredients. Don't use an electric mixer for this.
- Generously butter your loaf pan (see point 1) and pour the batter into it.
- Bake on the middle shelf of your oven at 180°C/355°F for 60-65 minutes.
- Cool cake slightly after it has baked.
- Mix all ingredients for the glaze.

- Use a knitting needle and make plenty of wholes into the loaf and pour the glaze over the cake.

Nutrition Information

- Calories: 4455.7
- Cholesterol: 1591.8
- Saturated Fat: 135.8
- Sodium: 2670
- Fiber: 7.3
- Sugar: 353.8
- Total Carbohydrate: 556.8
- Total Fat: 229
- Protein: 59.9

72. Gluten Free Swiss Roll

Serving: 8 serving(s) | Prep: 20mins | Ready in:

Ingredients

- 4 eggs
- 1 cup sugar
- 1 cup gluten-free self-raising flour, sifted
- 2 tablespoons hot milk
- 1 tablespoon sugar, extra
- 3/4 cup jam
- 2 tablespoons icing sugar

Direction

- Heat oven to 180°C Grease a 25cm x 30cm Swiss Roll tin. Line the base of the tin with baking paper and grease the paper.
- Beat the eggs and sugar in a large bowl until pale and thick.
- Lightly fold in the flour.
- Drizzle the milk down the inside of the bowl and lightly fold through.
- Pour the mixture into the prepared tin and bake 10 - 12 minutes, or until golden and a metal skewer inserted into the centre comes out clean.
- Place a piece of baking paper on a board that is slightly larger than the Swiss Roll tin being used. Spread over it the extra 1 tablespoon of sugar.
- Turn the cake out, onto the paper. Peel off the original baking paper and discard the original paper. Roll up the cake with the new layer of baking paper.
- Cover the cake loosely with a clean tea-towel and transfer to a wire rack to cool.
- Gently unroll the cake, discard the baking paper, spread over the jam and roll back up again.
- Sift the icing sugar over the top and serve.

Nutrition Information

- Calories: 247.8
- Total Fat: 2.5
- Fiber: 0.3
- Sugar: 47
- Cholesterol: 93.5
- Protein: 3.4
- Saturated Fat: 0.9
- Sodium: 47.4
- Total Carbohydrate: 53.6

73. Leckerli

Serving: 24 bars | Prep: 30mins | Ready in:

Ingredients

- 1/2 cup honey
- 1/3 cup sugar
- 2 1/2 cups flour, unsifted all-purpose
- 4 teaspoons baking powder
- 1 teaspoon cinnamon
- 1 pinch nutmeg
- 1 pinch clove
- 2/3 cup almonds, sliced
- 3 tablespoons orange peel, candied, finely chopped

- 3 tablespoons lemon peel, candied, finely chopped
- 1 egg
- 2 tablespoons kirsch (or orange juice)
- milk
- candied red cherries, halved
- angelica (or candied citron peel cut in leaf shapes-optional)

Direction

- Combine honey and sugar in a small saucepan. Heat slowly, stirring constantly, until honey thins and sugar dissolves; cool slightly.
- Sift flour, baking powder, cinnamon, nutmeg and cloves into a large bowl.
- Add almonds, candied orange and lemon peels; mix to coat.
- Add cooled honey mixture, egg and kirsch to flour mixture; stir with wooden spoon until blended.
- Knead dough together with palm of hand until mixture cleans side of bowl; shape into ball; flatten slightly.
- Roll dough between two sheets of wax paper to a 13x9 inch rectangle, slightly less than 1/4 inch thick, keeping edges as even as possible.
- Remove top piece of wax paper; flip dough onto lightly greased cookie sheet; remove second piece of wax paper.
- Brush top lightly with milk.
- Bake in a moderate over (375 degrees F) for 15 minutes or until golden brown.
- Remove cookie sheet to wire rack.
- Trim edges of cookie dough; cut into 2-inch squares.
- Make GLAZE: Combine 1/2 cup granulated sugar and 3 Tbsps. water in saucepan. Cook about 5 minutes or until it registers 235 degrees F on candy thermometer.
- Brush Glaze quickly over warm Leckerli. (Do not make glaze until Leckerli are out of the oven or it will harden.)
- Decorate with candied red cherry halves and angelica leaves. (Glaze will harden and turn white.).

Nutrition Information

- Calories: 107.2
- Total Fat: 2.3
- Saturated Fat: 0.2
- Sodium: 77.1
- Sugar: 8.8
- Total Carbohydrate: 19.9
- Fiber: 1
- Cholesterol: 7.8
- Protein: 2.5

74. Magenbrot, Soft Gingerbread

Serving: 200 cookies | Prep: 2hours | Ready in:

Ingredients

- Dough
- 1 kg flour
- 1 kg sugar
- 1 tablespoon cinnamon, ground
- 1/2 teaspoon clove, ground
- 1 teaspoon ginger, ground
- 1/2 teaspoon nutmeg, ground
- 2 teaspoons baking soda
- 800 ml water, cold
- Glaze
- 800 g icing sugar
- 300 ml water
- 2 tablespoons margarine
- 1 teaspoon cinnamon, ground
- 700 g chocolate, cooking dark

Direction

- Preheat the oven at 190°C (heat and timing are basing it on convection oven).
- Mix well all the ingredients for the dough together.
- Cover your square mold of 30 to 40 cm with baking paper and smear your dough.
- Bake 30-40 minutes at 190°C.

- Remove tray from oven and store at least 8 hours.
- Cut the dough into rectangles of a size of about 2 cm by 3 cm.
- For the glaze melt at low temperature the chocolate in the water.
- Add all the remaining ingredients, mix well and keep warm.
- Dip your pieces of dough into the glaze, let drop on a grate.
- Transfer on a tray and let dry some hours. Turn once and let dry again.
- Store in an airtight containers.

Nutrition Information

- Calories: 71.9
- Sodium: 15.2
- Sugar: 8.9
- Total Carbohydrate: 13.9
- Protein: 1
- Total Fat: 2
- Fiber: 0.8
- Cholesterol: 0
- Saturated Fat: 1.2

75. Mandel Broetli (Almond Biscuits)

Serving: 50 serving(s) | Prep: 45mins | Ready in:

Ingredients

- 4 eggs
- 500 g icing sugar (confectioner's sugar)
- 2 tablespoons kirsch
- 1/2 teaspoon almond essence
- 1 pinch salt
- 550 g plain flour
- 100 g ground almonds

Direction

- Cream eggs and sugar.
- Add kirsch, almond essence, and salt.
- Add flour ground almonds and knead to a dough. (You may need a little extra flour).
- Roll out the dough to 1cm thick on a floured surface.
- Using cookie cutters, cut out shapes, make decorations on them using shortbread moulds (or use Anisbrötli Mödeli if you have them!).
- Place on baking paper on an oven tray.
- Bake at 160 degrees Celsius for 20 minutes. The biscuits should not brown but stay light in colour.

Nutrition Information

- Calories: 106.5
- Total Fat: 1.6
- Saturated Fat: 0.2
- Fiber: 0.6
- Total Carbohydrate: 20.9
- Protein: 2.4
- Sodium: 9.1
- Sugar: 10
- Cholesterol: 16.9

76. Raspberry Chocolate Hazelnut Tart

Serving: 8 serving(s) | Prep: 15mins | Ready in:

Ingredients

- 2 cups hazelnuts (toasted and skins rubbed off)
- 6 tablespoons brown sugar, packed
- 1/4 teaspoon cinnamon
- 1/4 cup unsalted butter, melted
- 3/4 cup whipping cream
- 6 ounces bittersweet chocolate or 6 ounces semisweet chocolate, chopped
- 1 pint fresh raspberry
- 1/4 cup seedless raspberry jam

Direction

- Preheat the oven to 325°.
- In a food processor, finely grind the nuts, then add the sugar and cinnamon.
- Add the butter and process until moist clumps form.
- Press into a tart pan with a removable bottom.
- Bake until golden brown and firm to touch, 5-10 minutes (watch closely).
- Transfer to a rack and allow to cool completely.
- Bring the cream to a simmer in a heavy saucepan.
- Remove from the heat.
- Add the chocolate and stir until melted and smooth.
- Pour the mixture into the crust. Chill until set, about 1 hour.
- Arrange the raspberries on top.
- Stir the jam in a heavy small saucepan over low heat until melted.
- Brush the melted jam over the raspberries.
- Garnish with a little whipped cream, or shaved chocolate and a sprig of fresh mint if you would like.

Nutrition Information

- Calories: 427.4
- Saturated Fat: 10.3
- Fiber: 6
- Sugar: 18.1
- Total Carbohydrate: 28
- Protein: 6.1
- Total Fat: 34.8
- Cholesterol: 45.8
- Sodium: 15.8

77. Riebeles (Swiss Fried Cornmeal Cakes)

Serving: 12 cakes, 3-4 serving(s) | Prep: 25mins | Ready in:

Ingredients

- 2 tablespoons butter, softened
- 2 cups milk
- 2 cups water
- 1 tablespoon vegetable oil
- 1 1/3 cups yellow cornmeal (about 8 ounces)
- 2 teaspoons salt
- 2 -6 tablespoons butter, as needed

Direction

- Using a pastry brush, spread the softened butter on the bottom and sides of an 8"x6" or 9"x6" shallow baking dish. Set aside.
- Place milk, water and oil in a heavy 3-4 quart saucepan.
- Bring to a boil over high heat.
- Add cornmeal in a slow, thin stream, stirring constantly, so that liquid continues to boil as cornmeal is absorbed.
- Reduce heat to low and simmer for 15-20 minutes, stirring frequently, until mixture is so thick that spoon will stand unsupported in center of pan.
- Spoon into buttered dish while hot, spreading it out and smoothing the top with a spatula.
- Cover and refrigerate at least 6 hours, or overnight.
- Using a pastry wheel or sharp knife, cut the chilled cornmeal into 2" squares and gently lift them out of the dish with a small metal spatula.
- Melt 2 tablespoons of butter in a large, heavy skillet over moderate heat.
- Add 4 or 5 of the cornmeal cakes to the pan and brown for 2-3 minutes on each side, turning gently with a spatula.
- Repeat with remaining cakes, adding more butter if necessary.
- Serve immediately.

Nutrition Information

- Calories: 476.2
- Fiber: 4
- Sugar: 0.4

- Cholesterol: 63.5
- Protein: 9.9
- Total Fat: 27.8
- Saturated Fat: 14.3
- Sodium: 1788.9
- Total Carbohydrate: 49.3

78. Rüebli Kuchen (Carrot Cake)

Serving: 1 loaf cake | Prep: 10mins | Ready in:

Ingredients

- 350 g flour (0.77 pounds)
- 15 g baking powder (0.5 ounces)
- 300 g sugar (0.66 pounds) or 300 g raw sugar (0.66 pounds)
- 2 teaspoons cinnamon
- 3/4 teaspoon cardamom
- 2 pinches clove powder
- 1 pinch salt
- 250 g carrots, shredded into small pieces (0.55 pounds)
- 1 lemon
- 250 g ground almonds (0.55 pounds)
- 4 eggs
- 200 g margarine (0.44 pounds)

Direction

- Put flour in a stir bowl.
- Add sugar, cinnamon, cardamom, clove powder and salt, mix well.
- Add carrots, almonds, lemon juice and small pieces of lemon skin, mix well.
- Beat eggs and add together with the margarine.
- Mix again and pour into baking tin.
- Bake for about 65 minutes at 180°C (355°F) in the pre-heated oven.
- Put marzipan carrots on top of the cake for decoration. (Marzipan is also referred to as marchpane or almond paste).

Nutrition Information

- Calories: 5741.7
- Saturated Fat: 49.7
- Sodium: 3696.5
- Fiber: 51.9
- Sugar: 324.2
- Total Carbohydrate: 662.8
- Cholesterol: 744
- Total Fat: 308
- Protein: 119.5

79. Schokoladeschaumden (Swiss Chocolate Puffs)

Serving: 20-24 serving(s) | Prep: 10mins | Ready in:

Ingredients

- 200 g superfine sugar (about 1 cup)
- 1 teaspoon white vinegar
- 1 egg white
- 1 tablespoon powdered chocolate milk mix (like Nesquik)
- 1 teaspoon cocoa powder

Direction

- Preheat oven to 250°F (120°C).
- In a medium bowl, beat egg white until stiff peaks form. Still beating, gradually add sugar and vinegar. The mixture must remain stiff. Add the chocolate powder and cocoa to the egg white mixture, and beat just until the chocolate and cocoa are fully incorporated into the egg white mixture.
- Place little spoonfuls on an ungreased cookie sheet. Bake at 250°F (120°C) oven for 15 to 16 minutes. Cool. Store in an airtight container.

Nutrition Information

- Calories: 3.9
- Total Fat: 0

- Saturated Fat: 0
- Fiber: 0.1
- Sugar: 0.6
- Total Carbohydrate: 0.7
- Cholesterol: 0
- Sodium: 3.5
- Protein: 0.2

80. Springerle Cookies

Serving: 60 cookies | Prep: 24hours | Ready in:

Ingredients

- 4 large eggs
- 3 cups flour
- 4 1/4 cups powdered sugar (1 pound)
- 1 tablespoon freshly grated lemon zest
- 1 teaspoon baking powder
- 1/2-1 teaspoon anise extract
- anise seed

Direction

- In large mixer bowl, beat eggs at high speed until thick lemon colored.
- Continue beating while adding sugar slowly; add flour, baking powder, lemon peel anise extract- beat together completely.
- On a well-floured board, roll out some of the dough with a plain rolling pin to about 1/2" thickness; lightly flour Springerle rolling pin roll it firmly across dough to impress patterns (try to keep dough about 1/2" thick).
- Cut cookies apart between patterns.
- Place cookies 1/2" apart on ungreased cookie sheets, and allow them to dry uncovered overnight (12 hours).
- When ready to bake, preheat oven to 250-300° place cookies 1/2" apart on lightly greased cookie sheets. Bake 25-30 minutes until firm but still white.
- Remove to wire racks to cool.
- Store cookies in a tightly covered container with some anise seeds.
- Flavour develops fully after about 2 weeks.

Nutrition Information

- Calories: 60.8
- Total Fat: 0.4
- Sodium: 11.1
- Fiber: 0.2
- Saturated Fat: 0.1
- Sugar: 8.3
- Total Carbohydrate: 13.3
- Cholesterol: 12.4
- Protein: 1.1

81. Sweet Ham And Swiss Sliders

Serving: 16 serving(s) | Prep: 15mins | Ready in:

Ingredients

- 16 white dinner style rolls, cut in half
- 24 slices honey-roasted ham
- 16 slices swiss cheese
- 1/4 cup mayonnaise
- 1 1/2 tablespoons Dijon mustard
- 8 tablespoons butter, melted
- 1 teaspoon onion powder
- 1/2 teaspoon Worcestershire sauce
- 1 tablespoon poppy seed
- 1/4 cup brown sugar

Direction

- Preheat oven to 400°.
- On a rimmed baking sheet place bottom half of dinner rolls and top with 1 1/2 slices of ham and 1 slice of Swiss cheese.
- Spread about 1 tsp of mayonnaise on each top-half of roll and place on top of ham and cheese.
- You want the rolls to be snug together, kissing just a bit so the sauce can soak up into all of the nooks and crannies.

- In a small bowl combine the mustard, melted butter, onion powder, Worcestershire sauce, poppy seeds, and brown sugar.
- Mix until combined and evenly pour over the assembled rolls.
- Cover with foil and refrigerate until ready to bake.
- Bake covered with foil for 10 minutes, remove the foil and bake for an additional 5-10 minutes or until the tops are browned, and cheese is good and melted.

Nutrition Information

- Calories: 393.7
- Saturated Fat: 9.5
- Sodium: 816.2
- Sugar: 4.8
- Protein: 21.1
- Total Fat: 17.3
- Fiber: 1.5
- Total Carbohydrate: 38.4
- Cholesterol: 50.4

82. Sweet Onion And Swiss Phyllo Roll Ups

Serving: 6 rolls, 8-10 serving(s) | Prep: 25mins | Ready in:

Ingredients

- 8 ounces cream cheese, softened
- 2 cups swiss cheese, shredded
- 2 onions, chopped
- 3 garlic cloves, minced
- 1/4 cup butter
- 1/2 teaspoon dried thyme leaves
- 1/8 teaspoon pepper
- phyllo dough, thawed
- 1/3 cup butter, melted

Direction

- Preparation:
- In medium bowl, mix cream cheese and Swiss cheese. Set aside. In heavy skillet, sauté onions, thyme, and pepper in 1/4 cup butter until very soft and beginning to brown, 10-15 minutes. Stir in garlic and cook another 1 minute. Cool 20 minutes. Mix together onion mixture and cheese mixture and refrigerate for 30 minutes.
- Place one sheet filo dough on work surface. Brush with melted butter. Lay another sheet on top, brush with butter, and put one more sheet on top.
- Take the onion mixture and form a roll about 1 inch in diameter down one long edge of the stacked filo. Roll up carefully and place on cookie sheet. Brush thoroughly with more butter. Repeat with remaining filo and filling, making six rolls total. I place three rolls on each cookie sheet. Cover well with plastic wrap and chill overnight.
- When ready to bake, preheat oven to 375 degrees F and remove the rolls from the refrigerator. Bake for 10-17 minutes or until rolls begin to brown and cheese filling melts. Let stand 5 minutes, then, using a very sharp knife, cut rolls into 1" pieces. Let cool for 5-10 minutes, then serve. The onion filling right out of the oven is super-hot. Serves 8-10 - or 4-6, at my parties!
- You can also freeze these rolls. Wrap well in freezer wrap, label, and freeze up to 3 months. To bake frozen rolls, place rolls on cookie sheets and bake at 375 degrees F for 15-23 minutes or until the rolls are beginning to brown and crisp and cheese melts. Proceed as directed above.

Nutrition Information

- Calories: 333.5
- Total Fat: 30.8
- Saturated Fat: 19.5
- Cholesterol: 91.6
- Sodium: 232.1
- Fiber: 0.4

- Sugar: 1.6
- Total Carbohydrate: 5.4
- Protein: 9.9

- Cholesterol: 0
- Saturated Fat: 0
- Sodium: 3.7
- Total Carbohydrate: 5.3

83. Swiss Alps Cookies

Serving: 45 cookies | Prep: 15mins | Ready in:

Ingredients

- 3 egg whites
- 1/4 teaspoon cream of tartar
- 3/4 cup granulated sugar
- 2 Toblerone chocolate bars, fruit nut finely chopped (100 g each)
- 3 tablespoons flour
- 3 tablespoons icing sugar

Direction

- Heat oven to 300°F
- Beat egg whites and cream of tartar in large bowl with mixer on high speed 3 to 5 minute or until soft peaks form.
- Beat in granulated sugar, 1 tablespoons at a time, until stiff peaks form.
- Mix chocolate and flour; gently stir into egg whites.
- Drop tablespoonfuls of egg white mixture, 1 inch apart, onto 2 parchment paper-covered baking sheets.
- Bake in top and bottom thirds of oven 24 to 26 minute or until light golden brown, rotating baking sheets after 12 minute
- Transfer to wire racks; cool completely.
- Sprinkle with icing sugar.

Nutrition Information

- Calories: 22.2
- Total Fat: 0
- Fiber: 0
- Sugar: 4.9
- Protein: 0.3

84. Swiss Apple Tart Apfelwähe

Serving: 6 serving(s) | Prep: 1hours30mins | Ready in:

Ingredients

- Pastry
- 1 1/2 cups all-purpose flour
- 1/8 teaspoon salt
- 3/4 cup butter, well chilled
- 1/2 cup extra finely granulated sugar
- 1 teaspoon grated lemon rind
- 1 large egg, lightly beaten
- Filling
- 2 lbs of a tart baking apples
- 3 ounces ground almonds
- 1 grated lemon, rind of
- 3 teaspoons extra finely granulated sugar
- 2 teaspoons ground cinnamon
- 1 ounce butter, cut into flakes (or use a butter curler to produce this much butter in short curls)
- Custard
- 8 fluid ounces whipping cream
- 1 teaspoon cornstarch
- 2 large eggs
- 1 egg yolk
- 4 tablespoons extra finely granulated sugar

Direction

- Sift the flour and sugar together into a large mixing bowl. Coat the butter with flour from the bowl to make it easier to handle, and grate it directly onto the flour, using the coarse blade of a cheese grater. As you grate the butter, mix the flakes together with the flour occasionally, using your fingertips, before grating more.

- Add the sugar and lemon rind. Using two round-bladed knives, cut the butter into the flour until the mixture resembles cornmeal.
- Mix the egg lightly with a fork and pour over the flour mixture. Using the fork, mix the egg into the flour mixture until well distributed. Then, using your hand, pull the dough gently together into a ball. Knead lightly and briefly on a floured board until the dough forms a cohesive mass. Pat into a flat round and wrap tightly in Saran wrap / plastic wrap / cling film. Refrigerate for at least an hour before using.
- Roll the dough out just thin enough to be about an inch and a half wider than the 10-12" tart pan, and either fold it in two for the move into the pan, or drape it over the rolling pin and move it that way. Carefully tuck the dough down so that it is flat both against the pan's bottom and the fluted sides. Press it gently against the fluting: then trim it off flat by rolling the rolling pin over the top edge. Prick the bottom of the crust-to-be with a fork.
- Preheat the oven to 375°F.
- Sprinkle the bottom of the pastry-lined pan/tin with the ground almonds. Combine the cinnamon, sugar and lemon zest in a small bowl.
- Peel, core and quarter the apples. Slice them very thin (you may want to use a mandoline-type vegetable slicer for this), toss them together with the cinnamon-sugar-zest mixture, and then arrange them in concentric circles on top of the ground almonds. Flake the butter on top.
- Mix the cornstarch well with about three tablespoonsful of the cream: then add this to the rest of the custard ingredients and mix well.
- Put the pastry in the oven and bake for fifteen minutes.
- When this time has elapsed, stir up the custard ingredients well one more time, then pour enough custard into the pastry to fill it to the top.
- Close the oven and bake for another 30 minutes. (If the pastry was showing too much browning at the 15-minute stage, you might want to decrease the heat just a little.)
- At the end of the 30 minutes, wiggle the pan a little to make sure that the custard's set. If it is, remove and allow to cool on a rack. If it isn't, give it another five or ten minutes, but no more. The custard usually puffs up while baking: when it collapses after you remove it from the oven, don't worry -- it's supposed to do that.
- The apfelwähe can be served hot, warm, or cold. Add whatever sides you prefer with an apple dessert -- pouring cream, more custard, a sharp cheese.

Nutrition Information

- Calories: 787.1
- Sugar: 38.4
- Total Fat: 52.3
- Sodium: 339.7
- Fiber: 7.9
- Total Carbohydrate: 73.9
- Cholesterol: 246.3
- Protein: 11.5
- Saturated Fat: 27.8

85. Swiss Apple And Bread Dessert

Serving: 4 serving(s) | Prep: 5mins | Ready in:

Ingredients

- 4 tablespoons butter
- 6 slices day-old white bread, crusts removed, cut in small pieces
- 3 green apples, peeled, cored, and thinly sliced
- 1/2 cup sugar
- 1/2 teaspoon cinnamon
- 1/2 cup raisins
- whipped cream, for serving (or vanilla sauce)

Direction

- Melt butter in a large skillet.
- Add bread pieces and brown well.
- Add apple slices.
- Cover and simmer until apples are soft, 10-15 minutes.
- Stir in sugar, cinnamon and raisins.
- Serve warm, topped with whipped cream or vanilla sauce.

Nutrition Information

- Calories: 424.3
- Protein: 3.9
- Sugar: 51.5
- Cholesterol: 30.5
- Sodium: 296.6
- Fiber: 5
- Total Carbohydrate: 77.5
- Total Fat: 13.1
- Saturated Fat: 7.6

86. Swiss Cherry Cheese Torte

Serving: 12 serving(s) | Prep: 30mins | Ready in:

Ingredients

- 1 package swiss chocolate cake mix or 1 package devil's food cake mix
- 3 eggs
- 1 1/3 cups water
- 1/3 cup oil
- 1 (21 ounce) can cherry pie filling
- 4 ounces cream cheese
- 2 teaspoons lemon juice
- 1 can creamy vanilla frosting

Direction

- Preheat oven to 350 degrees.
- Combine cake mix with oil, water and eggs.
- Bake in 2 (8 inch) greased and floured round cake pans for 35 to 40 minutes.
- Cool.
- Split each layer into 2 thin layers.
- For frosting cream vanilla frosting, cream cheese and lemon juice.
- Spread frosting over cake layers, then cherry pie filling on top of frosting.
- Continue, ending with pie filling on top.
- Store cake in refrigerator.

Nutrition Information

- Calories: 162.1
- Saturated Fat: 3.4
- Protein: 2.5
- Total Fat: 10.6
- Fiber: 0.3
- Sugar: 0.1
- Total Carbohydrate: 14.3
- Cholesterol: 63.3
- Sodium: 54.9

87. Swiss Chocolate Cherry Kuchen

Serving: 8 serving(s) | Prep: 10mins | Ready in:

Ingredients

- 1 cup butter or 1 cup margarine
- 1/2 teaspoon baking powder
- 4 unsweetened chocolate squares, broken
- 1/2 teaspoon salt
- 1 cup tart red cherries, canned, pitted, drained
- 2 cups sugar
- 4 eggs, beaten
- 2 teaspoons vanilla
- 2 cups sifted all-purpose flour
- 1 cup heavy cream, whipped

Direction

- Place butter and chocolate in medium bowl or glass measure; cover, melt in microwave oven 2 to 3 minutes until chocolate is melted.
- Mix well.
- Beat sugar gradually into eggs until fluffy.

- Beat in chocolate mixture.
- Mix and sift dry ingredients, add to chocolate egg mixture, beat well.
- Stir well drained cherries and vanilla into batter.
- Mix well.
- Divide batter evenly between 2 well sprayed 9 inch layer cake pans.
- Cover with wax paper.
- Cook 1 layer in 350F preheated oven 9 to 10 minutes, turning dish a quarter turn every 2 minutes.
- Let stand 10 minutes before turning out.
- Repeat with second layer.
- When cold, decorate each layer with whipped cream; cut in wedges to serve.

Nutrition Information

- Calories: 734.6
- Saturated Fat: 27
- Sodium: 422.7
- Cholesterol: 194.8
- Protein: 9.3
- Total Fat: 44.4
- Fiber: 3.6
- Sugar: 52
- Total Carbohydrate: 81.8

88. Swiss Chocolate Mousse

Serving: 2-4 serving(s) | Prep: 10mins | Ready in:

Ingredients

- 100 g tolberone chocolate candy bars, chopped
- 2 eggs, separated
- 1/2 cup thickened cream (whipped cream)

Direction

- 1) Melt chocolate in a large bowl over hot water.
- 2) Use a wooden spoon to mix in the egg yolks, one at a time; beat until smooth and thick.
- 3) Fold in whipped cream, then softly beaten egg whites.
- 4) Spoon the mixture into individual serving dishes, refrigerate for several hours or until firm.
- 5) Decorate with extra whipped cream, strawberries and chocolate curls if desired.

Nutrition Information

- Calories: 544.3
- Sugar: 26
- Total Carbohydrate: 31.7
- Fiber: 1.7
- Cholesterol: 279
- Protein: 11.3
- Total Fat: 41.6
- Saturated Fat: 24.5
- Sodium: 133.1

89. Swiss Honey Cake (Lebkuchen)

Serving: 1 batch | Prep: 20mins | Ready in:

Ingredients

- 1 cup honey
- 1/2 cup strong brewed coffee
- 1 cup cream
- 2 tablespoons kirsch
- 2/3 cup sugar
- 1 teaspoon nutmeg
- 1 teaspoon crushed anise seed
- 2 teaspoons cinnamon
- 4 cups flour (approximately)
- 1 1/2 teaspoons baking powder
- 1 teaspoon baking soda

Direction

- Blend honey with the coffee, cream, kirsch, sugar and spices.
- Sift the flour with the baking powder and soda; add it to the first mixture. Beat until smooth. The dough should be sticky.
- Put into a well-buttered 15x10 baking pan, spreading evenly to the corners. It should be about 1/4 to 1/2 inch thick.
- Bake at 350 for 30-40 minutes. Cut into bars.

Nutrition Information

- Calories: 4101.7
- Sodium: 1912.9
- Fiber: 17.8
- Sugar: 413.9
- Protein: 58.7
- Total Fat: 80
- Saturated Fat: 47.6
- Total Carbohydrate: 809.4
- Cholesterol: 265.3

90. Swiss Meringues (Meringues Schalen)

Serving: 6 serving(s) | Prep: 30mins | Ready in:

Ingredients

- 3 egg whites
- 1/4 teaspoon cream of tartar
- 3/4 cup granulated sugar
- 3/4 cup heavy cream, chilled
- 2 tablespoons powdered sugar
- 1 1/2 cups sliced strawberries

Direction

- Cover a cookie sheet with parchment paper.
- Beat egg whites and cream of tartar until foamy.
- Beat in the sugar, 1 Tbsp. at a time; continue to beat until stiff and glossy.
- Don't under beat!
- Using a 1/4 cup measure, drop small mounds of meringue batter onto the parchment.
- Try to get then into circular or oval shapes, using an icing spatula if needed.
- Bake at 225 F (preheated) for 1 hour, then turn off the oven and leave them inside for 1 hour without opening the oven door.
- Remove meringues from baking sheet and press an indentation in the base of each- using your thumb gently.
- Let cool to room temperature.
- Beat cream and powdered sugar together until stiff.
- Fold 1/4 of the sliced fruit into the whipped cream and use to fill the indentations on the cooled meringues.
- Decorate with remaining berry slices.
- Fill meringues only when ready to serve.

Nutrition Information

- Calories: 230.2
- Total Fat: 11.2
- Saturated Fat: 6.9
- Sugar: 29.4
- Total Carbohydrate: 31.4
- Cholesterol: 40.8
- Sodium: 39.1
- Fiber: 0.7
- Protein: 2.6

91. Swiss Milk Toffee

Serving: 20 squares | Prep: 10mins | Ready in:

Ingredients

- 2 lbs sugar
- 1 (218 g) can condensed milk
- 1 cup milk
- 1 cup water
- butter
- vanilla extract (optional)

Direction

- Grease one 7x11 inch baking pan and another of half the capacity.
- Put the sugar, condensed milk, milk and water into a large, deep saucepan (I use a pressure cooker pan). Add a walnut sized piece of butter.
- Heat the mix gently until all the sugar has dissolved, then bring to the boil.
- Reduce the heat and simmer gently, stirring occasionally. It needs to cook for up to an hour, but the colour will change from an unappealing beige to a golden caramel as it cooks, showing it's nearly ready.
- The toffee is ready when it reaches the soft ball stage. Use a candy thermometer, or drop a teaspoonful into some cold water.
- Half fill the sink with cold water and place the saucepan in it. Beat the toffee with a wooden spoon until smooth and thick. Stir in the vanilla, if using.
- Pour the toffee into the baking pans, getting all the really liquid part of it out of the saucepan. (As it sets, white "blooms" may appear. These are just milk solids (probably from the butter).
- Scrape the toffee that has stuck to the sides of the pan out with a metal spoon. This should give nuggets and flakes of toffee.
- When the toffee in the baking pans has set, score and cut into squares.

Nutrition Information

- Calories: 218.3
- Saturated Fat: 0.9
- Sugar: 51.2
- Total Carbohydrate: 51.9
- Cholesterol: 5.4
- Protein: 1.3
- Total Fat: 1.4
- Sodium: 20.1
- Fiber: 0

92. Swiss Plum Kuchen

Serving: 1 Very Beautiful Plum Cake | Prep: 20mins | Ready in:

Ingredients

- PASTRY DOUGH
- 3 cups flour
- 2/3 cup sugar
- 1/2 teaspoon salt
- 1 teaspoon baking powder
- 6 ounces butter
- 3 eggs
- ALMOND FILLING
- 2 cups blanched almonds
- 2/3 cup sugar
- 1 teaspoon almond extract
- 6 ounces butter
- 3 large eggs
- 1/2 cup flour
- 2 lbs plums
- 2/3 cup sliced almonds

Direction

- To make the dough, combine dry ingredients in bowl and mix.
- Add the butter cut into small pieces.
- Rub into the dry ingredients until mixture resembles fine breadcrumbs.
- Add eggs and mix until the dough forms a ball.
- Wrap the dough and chill.
- For the almond filling, using blender (or food processor), grind the almonds with the sugar until fine.
- Add the almond extract and butter and mix until smooth.
- Add eggs one at a time.
- Add flour and mix well.
- Roll the dough out on a floured surface and line a greased flan dish/tin.
- Trim the edge.
- Spread evenly with the filling.
- Remove stones from plums and slice into quarters.

- Arrange sliced plums cut side up on top of filling.
- Scatter the sliced almonds evenly over the plums.
- Bake at 300'F for about 45 minutes, until the dough is baked through and the filling is set.
- Cool in flan dish/tin on a rack.
- Serve sprinkled with icing-sugar (confectioner's sugar).

Nutrition Information

- Calories: 7989.4
- Sugar: 375.2
- Total Fat: 493.9
- Saturated Fat: 198.7
- Sodium: 4448.5
- Fiber: 60.7
- Total Carbohydrate: 775.7
- Cholesterol: 1847.5
- Protein: 167.2

93. Swiss Roll With Lemon Curd Filling

Serving: 1 17 inch roll, 17 serving(s) | Prep: 20mins | Ready in:

Ingredients

- 2 tablespoons butter, softened
- 2 tablespoons all-purpose flour
- 6 tablespoons sugar
- 4 eggs
- 1/2 cup self-rising flour
- lemon curd
- 2 tablespoons superfine sugar

Direction

- Preheat the oven to 400°F Using a pastry brush, coat the bottom and sides of an ll-by-17-inch jelly-roll pan with 1 tablespoon of softened butter. Line the pan with a 22-inch-long strip of wax paper, and let the paper extend over the ends of the pan.
- Brush the remaining butter over the paper, and sprinkle 2 tablespoons of all-purpose flour over it, tipping the pan to spread the flour evenly. Invert the pan and rap it sharply to remove the excess.
- With a whisk or a rotary or electric beater, beat the 6 tablespoons of sugar and the eggs together until the mixture is light and fluffy. A little at a time, sift the self-rising flour over the eggs, folding the mixture together gently but thoroughly with a rubber spatula. Do not overmix.
- Pour the batter into the jelly-roll pan and, with a spatula, spread it out evenly. Bake in the middle of the oven for 10 minutes, or until the top is a light golden color and the cake has begun to come away from the sides of the pan.
- Remove the cake from the oven and dust it evenly with the superfine sugar. Then turn it out on a sheet of wax paper and gently peel off the paper.
- Spread the top of the cake evenly with lemon curd and, starting at the long edge, roll it into a cylinder. Cool to room temperature. To serve, cut the cake into 1-inch slices and arrange the slices attractively on a plate.

Nutrition Information

- Calories: 68
- Saturated Fat: 1.2
- Sodium: 75.4
- Total Carbohydrate: 9.4
- Cholesterol: 47.4
- Total Fat: 2.5
- Fiber: 0.1
- Sugar: 6
- Protein: 1.9

94. Swiss Tobleronemousse

Serving: 4 serving(s) | Prep: 20mins | Ready in:

Ingredients

- 300 g toblerone chocolate
- 2 eggs
- 2 tablespoons icing sugar
- 2 cups whipping cream

Direction

- Chop the chocolate up coarsely and put into a bowl or double boiler.
- Set bowl over boiling water to melt the chocolate.
- Stir in the sugar and eggs until the sugar has dissolved and chocolate is melted and is lighter in color.
- Remove from heat.
- Whip the cream and fold into the chocolate mixture.
- Pour into 4 individual serving dishes or leave in bowl.
- Refrigerate for at least 3 hours before serving.

Nutrition Information

- Calories: 868.7
- Sugar: 12.6
- Total Carbohydrate: 37.9
- Cholesterol: 256
- Fiber: 12.4
- Protein: 15.2
- Total Fat: 85.6
- Saturated Fat: 52.5
- Sodium: 99

95. Swiss Walnut Pie (Engadiner Nusstorte Or Bündner Nusstorte)

Serving: 12-16 serving(s) | Prep: 1hours | Ready in:

Ingredients

- Pastry
- 350 g flour
- 200 g butter
- 200 g sugar
- 1/4 teaspoon salt
- 1 large egg, beaten
- Filling
- 200 g sugar
- 2 tablespoons water
- 250 g walnuts, coarsely chopped
- 150 ml heavy cream
- 3 tablespoons honey
- 1 egg white
- 1 egg yolk
- 2 tablespoons heavy cream

Direction

- Put all the ingredients for the pastry in a food processor and pulse until homogeneous; if necessary, add 1 or 2 tablespoon of water.
- With the dough, prepare 2 balls (2/3 and 1/3 respectively of the dough) and keep in the refrigerator for at least 30 minutes.
- Put the sugar, water and honey in a large heavy-based saucepan over medium heat. Stir gently to dissolve the sugar. Bring to the boil and let it continue to boil until it becomes a dark golden color. Stir from time to time.
- Add the nuts and the cream and stir the walnuts until well coated.
- Remove the saucepan from the heat and set aside to cool.
- Preheat the oven to 180°C Grease a 30 cm tin (heat and timing are basing it on convection oven).
- Roll out the larger ball between two sheets of cling film to a 34 cm circle and use it to line the tin of 30 cm square. Press the edges of the pastry against the side of the tin.
- Scrape the filling onto the pastry. Level the top as well as you can, but don't apply too much pressure, or you may tear the pastry and the filling will leak out. Fold the excess pastry inwards over the filling.

- Roll the second piece of pastry to a neat 29 cm circle. Moisten the edges of the pastry base in the tin with the egg white and position the second pastry circle on top of this. Use a fork to crimp and seal the edges Mix the reserved egg yolk with 2 tablespoon cream and brush the cover. Prick with a fork in several places. If you like, you can score a plaid pattern onto the surface with the fork.
- Bake for 35-40 minutes, or until golden brown. Leave to cool until lukewarm in the tin, then loosen the sides, release the clip and carefully transfer the pie to a wire rack to cool completely.

Nutrition Information

- Calories: 569
- Total Fat: 33.6
- Fiber: 2.2
- Cholesterol: 85.4
- Protein: 7.7
- Saturated Fat: 13.5
- Sodium: 185.1
- Sugar: 38.3
- Total Carbohydrate: 63.3

96. Swiss Zug Cherry Torte (Zuger Kirschtorte)

Serving: 1 cake, 12-16 serving(s) | Prep: 40mins | Ready in:

Ingredients

- Nut Layer
- 4 egg whites
- 1/2 cup powdered sugar (125g)
- 1/2 cup hazelnuts, ground (100g)
- 2 tablespoons cornstarch
- Biscuit Layer
- 3 egg yolks
- 3 egg whites
- 1/3 cup powdered sugar (75g)
- 1/2 cup flour (50g)
- 1/2 cup cornstarch (50g)
- 1/2 teaspoon baking powder
- 1/2 lemon, the zest of
- Butter Cream
- 2/3 cup butter (150g)
- 1 1/2 cups powdered sugar (150g)
- 1 egg yolk
- 4 tablespoons kirsch
- Finishing
- 4 tablespoons kirsch
- 1/2 cup hazelnuts, chopped (125g)
- 1 cup powdered sugar (100g)

Direction

- Nut Layer:
- Beat the egg whites until stiff and fold in half (1/4 cup) powdered sugar.
- Combine the remaining sugar, nuts and cornstarch, then fold this into the stiff egg whites.
- Bake two layers from the mixture, using a spring form at 350F for 10-15 minutes. (I trace 2 circles on parchment using the 9 or 8" spring form Place the parchment on a baking sheet Then I divide the batter between the 2 circles and lightly smooth to the lines of the circle then bake at 350 for 10 to 15 minutes. This is like a large macaroon and should be dry when done.
- Biscuit Layer:
- In a large bowl beat the egg yolks with 3 Tbsps. warm water until creamy then add ¼ cup of powdered sugar.
- In a medium bowl beat the egg whites with the remaining ¼ cup sugar until stiff.
- Fold the egg whites into the yolks and add the flour, cornstarch, baking powder and lemon zest to make a batter.
- Using the same sized spring form as for the nut layer, grease or line with parchment then add batter.
- Bake for 20 minutes at 350°F.
- Butter Cream:
- Beat the butter until creamy.

- Add the sugar and egg yolk and lastly the Kirsch.
- Divide into 3 portions.
- To Finish:
- Let all the layers cool.
- Spread 1/3 of the butter cream on the nut layer.
- Stack a biscuit layer on top.
- Sprinkle the biscuit layer with Kirsch then spread on the next 1/3 butter cream.
- Lay the second nut layer on top.
- Spread the remaining butter cream on top and on sides.
- Dust the top with the powdered sugar.
- Sprinkle the sides with nuts.
- Using a knife mark the top, powdered sugar in diamond.

Nutrition Information

- Calories: 362.4
- Total Fat: 18.5
- Saturated Fat: 7.5
- Sodium: 141
- Sugar: 33.3
- Total Carbohydrate: 45.8
- Cholesterol: 82.5
- Fiber: 1.4
- Protein: 5.3

97. Tangerine Cream With Brittle Topping

Serving: 6 serving(s) | Prep: 40mins | Ready in:

Ingredients

- Cream
- 300 ml tangerine juice (corresponding to juice of 6 to 8 Tangerines)
- 2 tablespoons lemon juice
- 80 g marzipan, greater
- 1 vanilla (seeds only)
- 1 tablespoon cornstarch
- 2 eggs (lightly beaten)
- 2 tablespoons sugar
- 200 ml heavy cream
- Brittle
- 20 g almonds, splits
- 2 tablespoons sugar
- 1/2 tablespoon water
- Candied Tangerine Zest
- 1 tangerine (zest only)
- 2 tablespoons sugar
- 100 ml water

Direction

- Cream:
- Mix well all ingredients for the cream (except heavy cream) together.
- Heat the mixture in a pot at low temperature stirring continuously until it binds.
- Take away from heat a continue stirring for 2 more minutes.
- Refrigerate until cool. In the meanwhile prepare brittle and candied tangerine zest.
- Wipe the heavy cream and bring it gently under the tangerine mix.
- Brittle:
- Roast in a nonstick pot the almonds by middle heat. Set aside tight on a baking foil.
- Heat sugar and water in the same pan until boiling point.
- Reduce to low heat und continue to stir until the caramel reaches a clear brown color (caramel).
- Spread the caramel on the roasted almonds.
- Wait 15 minutes or until cold.
- Candied Tangerine Zest:
- Cut the zest in very thin slices.
- Heat the slices, the sugar and the ware in a pot until translucent.
- Reduce the heat and continue stirring from time to time until dry.
- Place the zest, open on a baking foil and continue to dry by medium heat in the oven (let the oven lid slightly open) until desired.

- When dry, chop very finely and use for topping (or don't chop it if you want to keep some for different purposes).
- Finishing:
- Break the bridle and use as topping with the candied tangerine zest.
- Note: Total time includes cooling time.

Nutrition Information

- Calories: 223.2
- Fiber: 0.7
- Saturated Fat: 8.3
- Sodium: 49.7
- Sugar: 14.5
- Total Carbohydrate: 18
- Cholesterol: 107.3
- Protein: 3.7
- Total Fat: 15.8

---

98. Totenbeinli Swiss Hazel Nut Legs

Serving: 15-25 pieces | Prep: 15mins | Ready in:

Ingredients

- 55 g butter, softened
- 250 g white sugar
- 2 eggs
- 60 ml orange juice
- 1/2 teaspoon lemon zest, grated
- 7 g ground cinnamon
- 250 g flour
- 255 g hazelnuts, coarsely chopped

Direction

- Preheat oven to 165 degrees Celsius.
- Cream together butter and sugar until light and fluffy. Beat in the eggs one at a time, mixing well after each addition, then stir in the orange juice, lemon zest, and cinnamon.
- Fold in the flour and hazelnuts, mixing just enough to evenly combine. Form into 1/2 inch by 3 inch sticks, and place onto a baking sheet 1 inch apart.
- Bake in preheated oven until brown around the edges, about 15 minutes. Cool completely on a wire rack before serving.

Nutrition Information

- Calories: 221.8
- Saturated Fat: 3
- Cholesterol: 32.6
- Sugar: 1.5
- Total Carbohydrate: 17.1
- Protein: 5.5
- Total Fat: 15.5
- Sodium: 35.9
- Fiber: 2.6

---

99. Warm Chicory Salad With Sweet Garlic, Croutons, Bacon Roqu

Serving: 6 serving(s) | Prep: 25mins | Ready in:

Ingredients

- The Sweet Garlic
- 20 garlic cloves, peeled
- 1 cup milk
- 1 tablespoon sugar
- 2 tablespoons clarified butter
- salt
- fresh ground pepper
- The Croutons and Bacon
- 1/2 lb thick slab bacon, cut into 1/2-inch cubes
- 1 cup bread, crust removed, cut in 1/2-inch cubes
- 3-4 tablespoons rendered bacon fat
- The Mustard Dressing
- 1 shallot, finely diced
- 1 tablespoon Dijon mustard
- 2 tablespoons red wine vinegar

- 5 tablespoons extra virgin olive oil
- 1 pinch salt
- 1/4 teaspoon fresh ground pepper
- The Salad
- 1 head chicory lettuce, wash and dried (curly endive)
- 1/2 cup Roquefort cheese, crumbled
- fresh ground pepper

Direction

- To Prepare the Sweet Garlic: Place the garlic and milk in a heavy saucepan over medium-high heat, and bring the milk to a boil.
- Boil for 3 minutes.
- Remove from the heat.
- Discard the milk, reserving the garlic.
- Combine the sugar and butter over medium heat.
- Add the garlic and cook until the cloves are soft and lightly caramelized.
- Season with salt and pepper.
- Set the sweet garlic aside.
- To Prepare the Croutons and Bacon: Preheat the oven to 350°F.
- Meanwhile, fry the bacon in a skillet until it is crisp but not dry.
- Remove from the heat and place the bacon on paper towels.
- Pour off all but 3 to 4 tablespoons of the rendered bacon fat.
- Add the cubed bread to the pan and toss to coat.
- Season with salt and pepper and transfer the bread cubes to a baking sheet.
- Bake for 5 minutes, or until they are lightly browned.
- Set aside.
- To Make the Dressing: Mix the shallots, mustard, and vinegar together.
- Gradually whisk in the olive oil until the liquid is well blended.
- Season with salt and pepper.
- Set aside.
- To Serve: Tear the chicory leaves into small pieces.
- Place them in a serving bowl and set aside at room temperature.
- Heat the bacon in a small, heavy-bottomed skillet over medium-high heat.
- Add the croutons and then the dressing.
- Toss for 2 seconds, pour it over the salad greens, and toss thoroughly.
- (Don't overcook the dressing or the mustard will lose its flavor.) Serve the salad on individual plates, topped with crumbled Roquefort cheese, sweet garlic, and freshly ground pepper to taste.

Nutrition Information

- Calories: 380.8
- Sodium: 430.6
- Fiber: 0.5
- Sugar: 2.5
- Total Carbohydrate: 12.1
- Protein: 7.2
- Total Fat: 34
- Saturated Fat: 10.7
- Cholesterol: 41.6

100. Zimtsterne, Cinnamon Stars

Serving: 50 cookies, 20-25 serving(s) | Prep: 30mins | Ready in:

Ingredients

- 3 large egg whites
- 1 pinch salt
- 250 g powdered sugar
- 1 1/2 tablespoons cinnamon (or a little more, if you want)
- 1/2 tablespoon lemon juice
- 350 g ground almonds

Direction

- Beat egg whites with salt until stiff.

- Add the powdered sugar and mix.
- Keep 1 dl of the mixture as frosting.
- Add the rest of the ingredients and mix well.
- Roll the dough out in a ziploc bag, that's cut open (cut the two side seams so the two parts are held together only at the bottom) Cut out stars or whatever other shapes you want.
- Bake for 3-5 minutes in a preheated oven at 450°F.
- When cookies are still warm, dip one side of cookies in frosting.

Nutrition Information

- Calories: 260.8
- Sodium: 16.7
- Fiber: 2.3
- Total Carbohydrate: 43.8
- Protein: 4.3
- Total Fat: 8.9
- Saturated Fat: 0.7
- Sugar: 40.1
- Cholesterol: 0

101. Zurich Vicarage Tart

Serving: 8 serving(s) | Prep: 15mins | Ready in:

Ingredients

- 200 g flour
- 70 g butter, unsalted
- 1 pinch salt
- 100 ml ice water
- 1 tablespoon vinegar
- FILLING 1
- 75 g almonds, ground
- 75 g hazelnuts, ground
- 1 egg
- cinnamon, ground
- 50 g sugar
- 100 g apples, grated
- FILLING 2
- 800 g apples, peeled and halved
- 100 g raspberry jam

Direction

- In a food processor place the flour, salt and butter. Blitz until butter just combined. Add water and vinegar with motor running until the pastry just comes together.
- Turn out on lightly floured bench and gently mould into a disk. Place in fridge for 30mins.
- Roll out and line a 24 cm wide flan ring with the pastry.
- Mix the ingredients for the filling 1 together and spread on the base of the flan ring.
- Cover the filling with the thinly sliced apple halves (allowing space for the jam to penetrate). Use half the jam to spread over the sliced apples.
- Cook for 10 minutes in a hot oven, 200°C.
- Remove from the oven and cover the apples with the remaining raspberry jam and bake for a further 15-20 minutes.

Nutrition Information

- Calories: 434.1
- Saturated Fat: 5.7
- Fiber: 6.8
- Cholesterol: 42
- Total Fat: 20.2
- Sodium: 133
- Sugar: 29.8
- Total Carbohydrate: 59.9
- Protein: 7.7

Chapter 4: Swiss Holiday Event Recipes

***

102. Aussie Swiss Chicken

Serving: 4 serving(s) | Prep: 20mins | Ready in:

Ingredients

- 4 chicken breast fillets, skin removed (about 200g each)
- seasoned all-purpose flour
- 90 g butter
- 1 garlic clove
- 3/4 cup dry white wine
- 1 teaspoon French mustard
- 1/2 cup cream
- 3 shallots or 3 spring onions
- 4 slices ham
- 4 slices swiss cheese

Direction

- Dust chicken breasts with the seasoned flour.
- Heat the butter in frying pan; add crushed garlic and chicken; sauté gently until chicken is lightly golden brown.
- Add wine; bring to the boil.
- Reduce heat; simmer covered 20 minutes or until chicken is tender; remove chicken from the pan.
- Trim ham and cheese to approximately same size as chicken.
- Put a slice of ham on each chicken fillet, then top with cheese.
- Put on a heatproof serving dish.
- Cook in a moderate oven, uncovered, for 10 minutes or until the cheese has melted.
- While chicken is in oven, bring liquid to the boil; boil uncovered until approximately a half a cup of liquid remains in pan.
- Reduce heat, add cream, chopped shallots and mustard; stir until combined.
- Season with salt and pepper.
- Pour sauce over chicken.

Nutrition Information

- Calories: 402.5
- Total Fat: 35.2
- Sodium: 196.9
- Fiber: 0
- Total Carbohydrate: 6.3
- Protein: 8.8
- Saturated Fat: 22.2
- Sugar: 0.8
- Cholesterol: 107

103. Fondue For Crusty French Bread

Serving: 25 serving(s) | Prep: 10mins | Ready in:

Ingredients

- 1 lb sharp cheddar cheese, grated to melt faster
- 2 cups sour cream
- 1 jar lawry's garlic spread ("whole" jar WOW!)
- 2 cans campbells cream of shrimp soup

Direction

- Place cheese, soup and garlic spread in heavy pan and heat till melted.
- Add sour cream till mixed and hot.
- Transfer to fondue pot and serve with French/sourdough bread cubes.
- Fills fondue pot.

Nutrition Information

- Calories: 130.1
- Protein: 5.6
- Total Fat: 10.9
- Saturated Fat: 6.9
- Sodium: 312.3
- Fiber: 0.1
- Sugar: 0.1
- Total Carbohydrate: 2.6
- Cholesterol: 30.3

104. German Country Style Sourdough Rye Bread With Caraway Seeds

Serving: 14 Slices - Medium Loaf | Prep: 12hours | Ready in:

Ingredients

- Overnight Sourdough Sponge
- 50 g strong white bread flour
- 1/2 teaspoon fast-rising active dry yeast
- 3 tablespoons water
- 1 tablespoon milk
- Bread
- 250 ml tepid water
- 2 tablespoons caraway seeds
- 225 g rye flour
- 2 teaspoons salt
- 2 tablespoons sugar
- 225 g strong white bread flour
- 1 1/4 teaspoons fast-rising active dry yeast

Direction

- To make the sourdough Sponge.
- Mix all the ingredients together to make a smooth paste, cover with a tea towel and leave to ferment overnight at room temperature, for between 8 to 12 hours.
- To make the bread.
- When you are ready to make the bread, pour the water into the bucket, followed by all of the sourdough sponge and then add the caraway seeds.
- Then, add in this order: rye flour, salt, sugar and then the white bread flour.
- Finally sprinkle the dried yeast over the top and fit the bucket into the bread machine/maker.
- Set to the rapid wholemeal setting, for a medium sized loaf (750g) with the crust setting of your choice.
- Once the bread has cooked - take it carefully out of the bucket and leave to cool on a wire cooling rack. Remove the paddle if it is still in the bread before slicing.
- Serve with soups, hams, cold meats, cheese and pickles or make sandwiches of your choice.

Nutrition Information

- Calories: 140.7
- Total Fat: 0.7
- Saturated Fat: 0.1
- Cholesterol: 0.1
- Protein: 4
- Sodium: 334.4
- Fiber: 3.4
- Sugar: 2
- Total Carbohydrate: 30

105. Grittibanzen Christmas Bread Men

Serving: 6-10 serving(s) | Prep: 20mins | Ready in:

Ingredients

- 4 -4 1/2 cups flour
- 4 teaspoons active dry yeast
- 2 teaspoons salt
- 1 1/4 cups warm milk
- 3 1/2 tablespoons melted butter, cooled
- 1 egg
- 4 teaspoons sugar
- egg yolk, for brushing the dough

Direction

- Sift the flour into a mixing bowl and make a well.
- Add the yeast and warm milk. Mix yeast and milk and cover the bowl with a damp kitchen cloth and let it rest for 15 minutes.
- Add the remainder of the ingredients (except egg yolk) and mix together to make a soft dough (if too stiff add a bit of warm milk, if

too wet add some flour). Knead for 2-3 minutes.
- Cover with a damp kitchen towel and put in a warm place to rise for 45 minutes.
- Punch down. Shape into santas, decorate with raisins, chocolate, almonds, sugar, etc.
- Brush with egg yolk.
- Let rise again until doubled.
- Bake in a preheated 400 oven for about 20-25 minutes (or more or less) depending upon how big the men are. Done when golden brown.

Nutrition Information

- Calories: 426.7
- Protein: 12.5
- Saturated Fat: 5.8
- Sodium: 874.1
- Sugar: 3.1
- Total Fat: 10.4
- Fiber: 3
- Total Carbohydrate: 69.9
- Cholesterol: 55.9

106. Gurkensalat (Cucumber Relish Salad)

Serving: 4 serving(s) | Prep: 5mins | Ready in:

Ingredients

- 2 medium cucumbers
- 1/8 teaspoon pepper
- 1 1/2 tablespoons sugar
- 1/2 cup sour cream
- 1/2 tablespoon cider vinegar
- 1 tablespoon fresh parsley, minced
- 1/2 teaspoon salt

Direction

- Slice cucumbers paper-thin.
- Sprinkle slices with sugar, vinegar, salt and pepper.
- Marinate for 20 minutes, drain off liquid, and toss lightly with sour cream.
- Top with minced parsley.

Nutrition Information

- Calories: 97.3
- Total Fat: 5.8
- Fiber: 0.8
- Cholesterol: 14.9
- Protein: 1.6
- Saturated Fat: 3.4
- Sodium: 317.4
- Sugar: 8.2
- Total Carbohydrate: 11.1

107. Ham Swiss Crescent Ring

Serving: 8 serving(s) | Prep: 15mins | Ready in:

Ingredients

- 4 ounces cream cheese, softened
- 1/4 cup mayonnaise
- 1/2 lb quality deli ham, chopped
- 4 ounces shredded swiss cheese
- 1 1/2 teaspoons dried onion flakes
- 1/4 teaspoon dried thyme
- 1/4 teaspoon dried parsley
- 1/4 teaspoon salt
- 2 tubes crescent rolls

Direction

- Preheat oven to 375°F.
- Combine all ingredients (except rolls) in a bowl. I use an electric mixer to get it well blended.
- Open the crescent tubes and separate each roll into 4 rectangles. On a parchment lined or nonstick baking sheet lay the rectangles out to

form a circle. There are images here: https://www.pinterest.com/pin/121034308711924287/.
- Place filling in a ring shape on top of the dough circle. Fold the dough over to cover the filling.
- Bake for 20 minutes or until crescent dough looks done.

Nutrition Information

- Calories: 255.1
- Fiber: 1.3
- Total Fat: 15.3
- Sugar: 2.3
- Total Carbohydrate: 17.4
- Cholesterol: 59.3
- Protein: 11.8
- Saturated Fat: 6.8
- Sodium: 682.6

108. Jolly Baby Swiss Spread

Serving: 1 crock | Prep: 10mins | Ready in:

Ingredients

- 8 ounces baby swiss cheese
- 3 tablespoons mayonnaise
- 1/3 cup chopped onion
- 1/2 teaspoon fresh ground pepper
- 4 ounces crumbled crisp bacon (about 6 slices)

Direction

- Chop Baby Swiss finely in food processor. Add mayonnaise, onion and pepper and process until smooth. Stir in bacon by hand. Spread in mini crock (or other decorative dish) and refrigerate at least 1 hour before serving. Serve with breadsticks, crackers, French bread, apple or pears, or raw vegetables.

Nutrition Information

- Calories: 1673
- Total Fat: 125.4
- Fiber: 1.2
- Sugar: 8.1
- Total Carbohydrate: 30.1
- Cholesterol: 345.2
- Saturated Fat: 58.2
- Sodium: 3371.7
- Protein: 104.3

109. Marché De Noël Vin Chaud French Spiced Mulled Wine

Serving: 4-5 serving(s) | Prep: 5mins | Ready in:

Ingredients

- 750 ml red wine (Beaujolais, Chinon, Bordeaux or Anjou)
- 4 cinnamon sticks
- 1 orange, zest of
- 1 lemon, zest of
- 4 tablespoons granulated sugar
- 6 cardamom pods
- 6 whole cloves
- 2 cinnamon sticks
- 1/3 cup cognac

Direction

- Wrap the cardamom pods and cloves in a piece of cheesecloth or muslin.
- Mix the rest of the ingredients, apart from the cognac, together in a large saucepan. Add the bag of spices. Bring the mixture to a gentle simmer over a low heat. Do not allow the wine to boil.
- The mulled wine is hot enough when the sugar has dissolved. Add the Cognac to the saucepan when the sugar has dissolved and ladle the mulled wine through a tea strainer (or colander) into punch cups, mugs or glasses.

Nutrition Information

- Calories: 204.9
- Total Fat: 0
- Sodium: 7.3
- Sugar: 13.7
- Saturated Fat: 0
- Fiber: 0
- Total Carbohydrate: 17.4
- Cholesterol: 0
- Protein: 0.1

110. Microwave Gruyère Fondue

Serving: 8 serving(s) | Prep: 1mins | Ready in:

Ingredients

- 1 garlic clove, halved
- 4 cups gruyere cheese, shredded (or 1/2 Gruye,re , 1/2 Swiss or emmenthaler)
- 3 tablespoons flour
- 1/8 teaspoon white pepper
- 1/8 teaspoon garlic powder
- 2 teaspoons Dijon mustard
- 1 cup dry white wine (such as Fendant)
- serve with
- 1 lb French bread or 1 lb sourdough bread, cut into bite-sized cubes

Direction

- Rub the inside of a 2 quart microwave-safe casserole dish with cut clove of garlic; then, combine cheese, flour and seasonings in dish, tossing to mix.
- Mix the mustard with the wine and microwave on High for 1-2 minutes (until hot).
- Stir wine mixture into cheese mixture.
- Microwave uncovered on Medium for 7-9 minutes (until smooth), stirring every 2 minutes.
- Serve with bread.

Nutrition Information

- Calories: 415.1
- Total Fat: 19.2
- Sodium: 542.4
- Sugar: 0.7
- Saturated Fat: 10.6
- Fiber: 1.8
- Total Carbohydrate: 32.9
- Cholesterol: 59.4
- Protein: 21.5

111. Mimi's The Comeback

Serving: 1 cocktail | Prep: 1mins | Ready in:

Ingredients

- 6 fluid ounces domane ste. michelle sparkling wine
- 1 fluid ounce peach schnapps

Direction

- In a champagne flute, add 1 ounce if peach Schnapps.
- Fill remainder of glass with chilled Domaine Ste. Michelle Sparkling Wine.

Nutrition Information

- Calories: 745.9
- Total Fat: 0
- Saturated Fat: 0
- Cholesterol: 0
- Protein: 0.6
- Sodium: 44.4
- Fiber: 0
- Sugar: 7
- Total Carbohydrate: 24.1

112. Mini Hot Ham Swiss Sandwiches

Serving: 12 sandwiches | Prep: 15mins | Ready in:

Ingredients

- 12 small egg buns
- 12 slices shaved deli ham
- 12 slices swiss cheese
- Sauce
- 1/2 cup butter
- 1 tablespoon horseradish
- 1 teaspoon dry mustard
- 2 tablespoons chopped green onions
- 1 tablespoon poppy seed

Direction

- Put ham and Swiss cheese on small buns.
- Spread with sauce.
- Put in baking dish; cover with foil.
- Bake at 350 for 30 minutes.

Nutrition Information

- Calories: 345.4
- Sugar: 3.2
- Cholesterol: 62.1
- Total Fat: 20.1
- Saturated Fat: 11.2
- Sodium: 696.7
- Fiber: 1.5
- Total Carbohydrate: 24.3
- Protein: 16.6

113. New Potatoes With Three Cheese Fondue

Serving: 20 serving(s) | Prep: 15mins | Ready in:

Ingredients

- 2 teaspoons olive oil
- 1/2 cup chopped onion
- 1 cup whipping cream, plus
- 2 tablespoons whipping cream
- 1 (8 ounce) package cream cheese, room temperature
- 1 cup freshly grated parmesan cheese (about 2 ounces)
- 1/2 cup packed grated gruyere cheese (about 1 1/2 ounces)
- 1/4 teaspoon ground nutmeg
- 1 lb unpeeled large red potatoes, cut into 1 inch pieces
- 6 cups water
- 1 teaspoon salt
- 1 tablespoon extra virgin olive oil
- 1 tablespoon chopped fresh parsley

Direction

- Heat oil in heavy medium saucepan over medium heat.
- Add onion; sauté until soft, about 4 minutes.
- Reduce heat to low.
- Add cream, cream cheese, Parmesan, and Gruyère.
- Whisk until smooth, about 3 minutes.
- Stir in nutmeg.
- Season with salt and pepper.
- Remove from heat.
- Combine potatoes, 6 cups water and salt in large saucepan.
- Bring to boil over high heat.
- Reduce heat to medium and cook until potatoes are just tender when pierced with skewer, about 6 minutes.
- Drain.
- Transfer potatoes to bowl.
- Add olive oil and parsley; toss to coat.
- Season to taste with salt and pepper.
- (Fondue and potatoes can be prepared 1 day ahead. Cover separately and refrigerate. Whisk fondue 5 minutes over medium heat until melted and smooth. Reheat potatoes in 350°F oven 10 minutes.) Place potatoes on platter.
- Spear each with skewer (48 6-inch skewers).

- Serve with warm fondue.

Nutrition Information

- Calories: 145.4
- Total Fat: 12.3
- Saturated Fat: 6.8
- Sugar: 0.9
- Sodium: 249.9
- Fiber: 0.5
- Total Carbohydrate: 5.1
- Cholesterol: 38.2
- Protein: 4.2

114. One Pot Swiss Steak With Mushrooms

Serving: 6 serving(s) | Prep: 20mins | Ready in:

Ingredients

- 2 tablespoons oil
- 2 tablespoons butter
- 1 1/2-2 lbs sirloin tip steaks (3-4)
- 2 medium onions, chopped
- 2 stalks celery, diced
- 1 large green bell pepper, seeded and chopped
- 1 -2 teaspoon dried chili pepper flakes (optional) or 1 jalapeno pepper, seeded and chopped, to taste (optional)
- 3 -4 teaspoons dried oregano
- 1 -2 tablespoon fresh minced garlic
- 2 small bay leaves (or use 1 large)
- 3 cups sliced mushrooms
- 2 (16 ounce) cans stewed tomatoes, with juice
- 1 -2 tablespoon beef bouillon powder (optional)
- 1 -2 tablespoon Worcestershire sauce
- salt and black pepper (to taste)
- 1 cup water, mixed with
- 2 tablespoons cornstarch (or use beef broth) (optional)

Direction

- Heat oil and butter in a large Dutch oven over medium heat.
- Add in 2 steaks at a time and brown on each side, remove to a plate.
- Continue with remaining steak/s and remove to a plate.
- Add more oil into the pot if needed.
- Add in onions, celery, bell pepper, chili flakes (if using) and dried oregano; saute stirring with a wooden spoon for about 3 minutes scraping up any browned bits on bottom of the pot.
- Add in garlic and bay leaves and saute for 2 minutes.
- Add in mushrooms, stewed tomatoes with juice, Worcestershire sauce and beef bouillon powder (if using) bring to a simmer over medium-high heat.
- Add the browned steaks back to the pot.
- Season with salt and black pepper to taste.
- Reduce heat to medium-low and cook covered for about 1-1/2 hours.
- If you wish to thicken the juice, remove the beef to a bowl or plate.
- Mix the water or beef broth with cornstarch until smooth and add into the simmering liquid, stir until thickened (about 2 minutes) then add in the steaks back to the pot.

Nutrition Information

- Calories: 380.4
- Saturated Fat: 8.9
- Fiber: 3.5
- Total Carbohydrate: 17.7
- Cholesterol: 95.4
- Sodium: 497.6
- Sugar: 9.2
- Protein: 26.5
- Total Fat: 23.4

115. Oven Baked Muesli

Serving: 8 cups | Prep: 0S | Ready in:

Ingredients

- 3 cups rolled oats
- 2 cups wheat germ
- 1/2 cup sesame seeds
- 1/4 cup pumpkin seeds
- 1/2 cup cashews, roughly chopped
- 1/2 cup almonds, roughly chopped
- 1/2 cup shredded coconut
- 1/4 cup olive oil
- 1/4 cup maple syrup
- 1 cup dried fruit, of your choice (try raisins, apricots, etc.)

Direction

- Preheat oven to 225 degrees. In a large bowl, combine all ingredients and stir together until well mixed.
- On a lightly oiled 9x13" pan, spread mixture evenly and bake for 1 hour, stirring every 15 minutes.
- Let cool and stir in optional dried fruit.
- Store in an airtight container.
- Makes about 8 cups.

Nutrition Information

- Calories: 507.6
- Saturated Fat: 5.7
- Sodium: 107.1
- Protein: 16.8
- Sugar: 9.7
- Total Carbohydrate: 52
- Cholesterol: 0
- Total Fat: 28.5
- Fiber: 9.6

116. Potato Gratin With Apple, Pancetta And Swiss

Serving: 6 serving(s) | Prep: 15mins | Ready in:

Ingredients

- 1 1/2 lbs Red Bliss potatoes, thinly sliced
- 2 large golden delicious apples, cored and thinly sliced
- 4 ounces pancetta, browned and crumbled
- 2 tablespoons snipped fresh chives
- 8 ouces cave-aged gruyere or 8 ounces mild swiss cheese, grated
- 8 ounces heavy cream
- salt
- pepper
- 2 tablespoons butter, cut into tiny cubes
- 1/8 teaspoon grated nutmeg
- aluminum foil, to cover

Direction

- Preheat oven to 350°F.
- Toss potatoes and apple in a large mixing bowl with salt, pepper, cheese, and half of the crumbled pancetta and chives.
- Place evenly into a buttered 9x12 rectangular casserole or baking dish.
- Top with remaining chives, crumbled pancetta, and cream.
- Dot top with butter and sprinkle with nutmeg.
- Cover with aluminum foil and bake until potatoes are tender, about 90 minutes.
- Remove foil and bake 15 minutes more.
- Let sit 10-15 minutes before serving.

Nutrition Information

- Calories: 289.7
- Total Fat: 18.9
- Total Carbohydrate: 29.5
- Cholesterol: 64.6
- Protein: 3.2
- Saturated Fat: 11.7
- Sodium: 70.1

- Fiber: 3.8
- Sugar: 9.3

117. Pretzels I

Serving: 12 serving(s) | Prep: 15mins | Ready in:

Ingredients

- 1 (1/4 ounce) package active dry yeast
- 4 cups unbleached flour
- 1 1/2 cups water (110-120 degrees)
- 1 large egg, beaten
- 1 teaspoon salt
- 1 dash coarse salt
- 1 tablespoon sugar

Direction

- Dissolve yeast in warm water.
- Add salt and sugar to yeast mixture.
- Blend in flour and knead dough until smooth, about 7 to 8 minutes.
- Cover and let dough rise until double in bulk.
- Punch down.
- Cut dough into small pieces and roll into ropes.
- Twist ropes into pretzel shapes and place on greased cookie sheet.
- Using a pastry brush, brush pretzels with egg and sprinkle with coarse salt.
- Allow pretzels to rise until almost double in bulk.
- Bake at 425°F.
- For 10 to 15 minutes or until browned.
- Best if eaten immediately.
- If not, store in airtight container.

Nutrition Information

- Calories: 163.6
- Sodium: 211.6
- Sugar: 1.2
- Cholesterol: 15.5
- Total Fat: 0.8
- Fiber: 1.3
- Total Carbohydrate: 33.1
- Protein: 5.1
- Saturated Fat: 0.2

118. Quatre Épices French Four Spice Mix From The Auberge

Serving: 60-75 grammes | Prep: 5mins | Ready in:

Ingredients

- 1 tablespoon white peppercorns
- 1 small whole nutmeg
- 10 cloves
- 1 cinnamon stick, about 2-inch
- 1 teaspoon ground ginger
- 1 tablespoon allspice berry, see below (optional)

Direction

- Put all of the ingredients in a spice mill or blender and process until evenly ground.
- Store in a cool, dark, dry place.
- Lasts for about 4 to 6 weeks without any loss of intensity of flavour.
- NB: If you are REALLY concerned about using this mix in sweet cooking, the white peppercorns can be substituted for the same amount of allspice berries!

Nutrition Information

- Calories: 0.5
- Fiber: 0
- Total Carbohydrate: 0.1
- Cholesterol: 0
- Sugar: 0
- Protein: 0
- Total Fat: 0
- Saturated Fat: 0

- Sodium: 0

119. Rösti (Bernese Fried Potatoes)

Serving: 4 serving(s) | Prep: 10mins | Ready in:

Ingredients

- 2 lbs potatoes
- 1 large onion
- bacon, cut into small cubes

Direction

- Parboil the potatoes, leaving their skins on.
- Peel, and grate coarsely.
- Lightly fry the onions, adding the bacon cut into small pieces and continue to fry until golden brown.
- Add the potatoes to the onion and bacon mixture.
- Turn carefully from time to time whilst frying, until the "Rösti" is crisp.

Nutrition Information

- Calories: 190.5
- Total Fat: 0.2
- Fiber: 5.5
- Sugar: 3.4
- Total Carbohydrate: 43.5
- Saturated Fat: 0.1
- Sodium: 14.8
- Cholesterol: 0
- Protein: 4.9

120. Savory Baked Onions With Swiss Cheese

Serving: 4 serving(s) | Prep: 20mins | Ready in:

Ingredients

- 4 medium yellow onions, peeled and halved
- 3 tablespoons olive oil
- salt pepper
- 2/3 cup low sodium beef broth
- 2 teaspoons soy sauce
- 1/4 teaspoon dried sage (rubbed between fingers to release the flavor)
- 3/4 cup grated swiss cheese or 3/4 cup gruyere cheese

Direction

- Set oven to 400 degrees.
- Grease a 2-quart shallow baking dish.
- Brush the tops of the onions with oil, then sprinkle with salt and pepper.
- Bake for about 40 minutes.
- In a small bowl whisk together the broth and soy sauce.
- Remove onions from oven; pour the beef broth mixture on top and around the baked onions.
- Return to oven and bake another 45 minutes basting about every 15 minutes.
- Sprinkle the sage and grated cheese over the onions; return to oven to about 5 minutes or until the cheese melts.

Nutrition Information

- Calories: 214.6
- Total Fat: 15.8
- Sodium: 210
- Fiber: 1.6
- Sugar: 5
- Total Carbohydrate: 12.4
- Cholesterol: 18.6
- Saturated Fat: 5
- Protein: 6.8

121. Schokoladen Torte (Chocolate Cake)

Serving: 10-12 serving(s) | Prep: 30mins | Ready in:

Ingredients

- 1 cup all-purpose flour
- 1 teaspoon baking powder
- 1/2 lb dark swiss chocolate (sweet chocolate)
- 1/2 cup butter or 1/2 cup margarine, at room temperature
- 1 cup sugar
- 5 eggs, separated
- 1 teaspoon vanilla extract
- sifted confectioners' sugar, for garnish (icing sugar)
- 1/2-1 cup prepared whipped cream, for garnish
- 12 hazelnuts or 12 berries, for garnish

Direction

- Place 9-inch springform pan on sheet of wax paper, use pencil to trace around bottom and cut out with scissors.
- Butter bottom and sides of pan; line bottom of pan with buttered wax paper circle.
- Preheat oven to 350°F.
- Sift flour and baking powder into small bowl.
- Coarsely grate chocolate on piece of wax paper and transfer to top pan of double boiler.
- Fill bottom pan of double boiler halfway with water; bring to boil over high heat.
- Reduce heat, set pan with grated chocolate on top of other pan, add butter and stir until melted and smooth (7 to 10 minutes).
- Add sugar; stir until melted (2 to 3 minutes).
- Transfer chocolate mixture to large mixing bowl.
- Using an electric mixer or mixing spoon, add egg yolks, one at a time, beating well after each addition.
- Add vanilla extract to mixture and mix well.
- Place egg whites to medium mixing bowl, and using clean dry mixer or whisk, beat until stiff.
- Using rubber spatula, fold in egg whites with chocolate mixture; transfer to prepared springform pan.
- Bake for 40 to 50 minutes or until toothpick inserted in center comes out clean.
- Cool torte on wire cake rack; remove sides of pan.
- Place 9-inch lace paper doily on top of cake; sift confectioners' sugar over it; remove doily.
- Pipe whipped cream dollops around edge of cake top and place a hazelnut or berry in each cream dollop.
- Serve with extra whipped cream.

Nutrition Information

- Calories: 363.9
- Total Fat: 24.3
- Total Carbohydrate: 37.1
- Saturated Fat: 14.4
- Sodium: 162.7
- Fiber: 4.1
- Sugar: 20.6
- Cholesterol: 119.7
- Protein: 7.6

122. Smoked Ham Salad On Gruyere Potato Coins

Serving: 36 coins | Prep: 15mins | Ready in:

Ingredients

- 2 long thin potatoes, cut into 1/8 inch thick slices
- 1 tablespoon olive oil
- salt freshly ground black pepper
- 1 cup shredded gruyere cheese (about 4 ounces)
- 1/2 lb lean smoked ham, finely chopped
- 3 tablespoons mayonnaise
- 1 scallion, finely chopped
- 1 tablespoon finely chopped cornichon

- 1 tablespoon finely chopped capers
- 1 teaspoon finely chopped tarragon
- 2 teaspoons Dijon mustard

Direction

- Preheat the oven to 350° and line a baking sheet with parchment paper or foil.
- Using a 2-inch round biscuit cutter, cut the potato slices into rounds.
- In a bowl, toss the potatoes with the olive oil and arrange them in a single layer on the baking sheet.
- Season lightly with salt and pepper, then sprinkle with the cheese.
- Bake the potato rounds for about 45 minutes, or until deep golden; let cool.
- Transfer the potato coins to paper towels.
- In a small bowl, combine the ham with the mayonnaise, scallion, Cornichons, capers, tarragon and mustard.
- Season with salt and pepper.
- Spoon the ham salad onto the potato coins and serve.

Nutrition Information

- Calories: 38.2
- Total Fat: 2.1
- Saturated Fat: 0.9
- Fiber: 0.3
- Sugar: 0.1
- Protein: 2.6
- Sodium: 133.3
- Total Carbohydrate: 2.2
- Cholesterol: 7.6

123. Swiss Chard Potato Soup

Serving: 6 serving(s) | Prep: 15mins | Ready in:

Ingredients

- 2 tablespoons butter
- 1 cup onion, chopped
- 1 bunch swiss chard, trimmed, leaves and stems chopped separately (to make about 6 cups of chopped leaves)
- 2 cups yukon gold potatoes, peeled, diced
- 4 cups chicken stock
- 1 cup milk
- salt freshly ground black pepper
- Garnish
- 2 tablespoons vegetable oil
- 1/4 cup swiss chard, thinly sliced

Direction

- Heat butter in a pot over medium heat. Add onions and Swiss chard stems and sauté for 2 minutes or until softened.
- Add potatoes, chicken stock and milk and bring to a boil.
- Simmer soup for 5 minutes; add Swiss chard leaves (reserving 1/4 cup for garnish) and simmer 5 minutes longer or until potatoes are very soft and chard is wilted.
- Puree soup in a blender or food processor (An immersion blender also works well). Season with salt and pepper to taste.
- Garnish:
- Heat oil in a small skillet over medium high heat. Working in batches, add Swiss chard (be careful, as it will pop and splatter oil) and fry for 1 to 2 minutes or until crisped.
- Drain on paper towels.
- Garnish soup with crinkled Swiss chard.

Nutrition Information

- Calories: 226
- Saturated Fat: 4.5
- Sodium: 425.2
- Fiber: 2.4
- Cholesterol: 20.7
- Total Fat: 12
- Sugar: 4.8
- Total Carbohydrate: 22.9
- Protein: 7.8

124. Swiss Chard And Leek Gratin

Serving: 5 serving(s) | Prep: 20mins | Ready in:

Ingredients

- 1 1/2 lbs swiss chard, large stems discarded
- 1 1/2 tablespoons extra-virgin olive oil
- 3 medium leeks, white and tender green parts only, sliced 1/4 inch thick
- salt
- 1 1/2 garlic cloves, minced
- 3 tablespoons unsalted butter
- 1/3 cup all-purpose flour
- 2 cups milk
- 1/4 cup gruyere cheese, shredded
- 1/4 cup parmigiano-reggiano cheese, shredded
- 1/8 teaspoon nutmeg, freshly grated
- black pepper, freshly ground

Direction

- In a large pot of boiling water, blanch the chard until wilted, about 1 minute. Drain the chard, squeeze it dry, and chop. Be sure to remove any excess moisture.
- Heat the oil in the pot. Add the leeks and a pinch of salt. Cover and cook over medium to medium low heat, stirring, until tender, 7 minutes. You know your stove -- if it cooks hot make it medium low, if it cooks low, make it medium. Uncover, add the garlic, and cook, stirring, until fragrant (about 2 minutes). Add the chard, season with salt to taste and remove from the heat.
- Preheat the oven to 425 degrees. Butter or grease a 2 qt casserole dish.
- In a large saucepan, melt the butter. Stir in the flour over moderate heat to form a paste. Gradually whisk 1/3 of the milk and cook, whisking, until the mixture starts to thicken. Repeat two more times with the remaining milk.
- Bring the sauce to a boil, whisking constantly. Reduce the heat to low and cook, whisking often, until thickened and no floury taste remains, about 10-15 minutes. Whisk in the cheeses and the nutmeg. Season with salt and pepper.
- Combine the sauce and leeks/chard mixture. Season with salt and pepper to taste.
- Transfer to the prepared casserole dish. Bake in the upper third of the oven for 25 minutes. Let rest for 10 minutes before serving to prevent burning your mouth.

Nutrition Information

- Calories: 288.7
- Total Fat: 17.9
- Fiber: 3.4
- Sugar: 3.7
- Total Carbohydrate: 24
- Saturated Fat: 9
- Sodium: 435.9
- Cholesterol: 40.8
- Protein: 10.6

125. Swiss Cheese Appetizer

Serving: 2 cups, 8-10 serving(s) | Prep: 10mins | Ready in:

Ingredients

- 8 ounces cream cheese, softened
- 8 ounces swiss cheese, shredded
- 2 tablespoons chopped green onions
- 1/2 cup mayonnaise
- 1/2 lb bacon, cooked crumbled

Direction

- Preheat oven to 350 degrees.
- Mix first 4 ingredients.
- Pour into pie plate or similar small baking dish.

- Bake for 30 minutes.
- Sprinkle the bacon on top.
- Bake for additional 5 minutes.
- Serve with crackers or crusty bread.

Nutrition Information

- Calories: 392.6
- Saturated Fat: 15.5
- Sodium: 486.5
- Cholesterol: 80.5
- Protein: 12.8
- Fiber: 0
- Sugar: 2.3
- Total Carbohydrate: 6.5
- Total Fat: 35.3

126. Swiss Cheese Cranberry And Pineapple Spread

Serving: 20 serving(s) | Prep: 10mins | Ready in:

Ingredients

- 8 ounces soft cream cheese with pineapple
- 6 ounces swiss cheese, shredded
- 1/2 cup dried cranberries
- 1 tablespoon orange rind
- 2 tablespoons dry sherry or 2 tablespoons apple juice
- 1/4-2/3 cup crushed pineapple, drained

Direction

- Preheat oven to 375 degrees.
- In a medium bowl, combine all ingredients.
- Spread in an ungreased 9" pie plate.
- Bake 14-16 minutes.
- Serve with apple or pear wedges and crackers.
- Can be made up to 12 hours in advance then baked.

Nutrition Information

- Calories: 36.9
- Saturated Fat: 1.5
- Sodium: 16.5
- Fiber: 0.2
- Total Carbohydrate: 1.4
- Protein: 2.3
- Total Fat: 2.4
- Sugar: 0.7
- Cholesterol: 7.8

127. Swiss Cheese And Ham Macaroni And Cheese

Serving: 6-8 serving(s) | Prep: 30mins | Ready in:

Ingredients

- 1/4 cup unsalted butter
- 5 tablespoons all-purpose flour
- 2 cups whole milk
- salt
- white pepper
- 1 pinch ground nutmeg
- 8 ounces dry elbow macaroni (uncooked)
- 8 ounces domestic swiss cheese, grated (2 cups grated)
- 8 ounces ham, cubed
- 1 cup frozen baby peas, thawed
- 1/4 cup grated parmesan cheese

Direction

- In a 2 to 3 quart sauce pot, melt butter over medium heat.
- Add the flour and stir for 2 minutes.
- Slowly add the milk, whisking to combine.
- Bring to a simmer, add the salt, white pepper and nutmeg.
- Reduce the heat to low and let sauce simmer slowly for 20 minutes.
- Meanwhile, preheat oven to 350 degrees and, on the stove top, cook the macaroni according to pkg. directions, drain and place in a large bowl.

- Remove the sauce from the heat, add the Swiss cheese and stir until it melts.
- Combine the sauce, cubed ham and peas with the drained macaroni.
- Pour the macaroni mixture into an 11x8x2" dish.
- Sprinkle the parmesan cheese on top and bake in preheated oven for 25 minutes.
- Let rest 5 minutes before serving.

Nutrition Information

- Calories: 526.8
- Sodium: 750.2
- Sugar: 7.1
- Protein: 30.1
- Total Fat: 25
- Saturated Fat: 14.7
- Fiber: 2.7
- Total Carbohydrate: 44.5
- Cholesterol: 86.7

128. Swiss Melt Mushroom Burgers

Serving: 6 serving(s) | Prep: 15mins | Ready in:

Ingredients

- 1 1/2 lbs hamburger
- 1/4 cup finely diced onion
- 2 eggs, lightly beaten
- 3/4 cup soft breadcrumbs
- 1/4 cup ketchup
- 1/2 teaspoon salt
- 1/8 teaspoon freshly ground black pepper
- 2 tablespoons butter
- 1/2 lb mushroom, sliced
- 6 slices swiss cheese
- 12 slices dark rye bread, toasted

Direction

- Mix well the first 7 ingredients (meat through to pepper) and form into twelve 1/4-inch thick patties.
- Melt the butter and saute the mushrooms lightly in it.
- Place on 6 of the patties.
- Top with remaining patties and seal edges.
- Broil or grill to desired doneness.
- Top with cheese.
- Place each patty on a slice of toasted bread and top with another slice of toast.

Nutrition Information

- Calories: 583
- Total Fat: 28.7
- Sugar: 6.4
- Protein: 40.4
- Saturated Fat: 13.3
- Sodium: 947.6
- Fiber: 4.4
- Total Carbohydrate: 39.9
- Cholesterol: 182.5

129. Swiss Meringue

Serving: 10 serving(s) | Prep: 15mins | Ready in:

Ingredients

- 2 egg whites (room temperature)
- 1/4 teaspoon cream of tartar
- 1/4 cup vanilla sugar (Flavored Sugar Flavored Sugar or Splenda)

Direction

- Preheat oven to 200 degrees. Line large baking sheet with parchment paper
- In a large grease-free mixing bowl beat the egg whites at a slow steady speed. When they are foamy add the cream of tartar. Gradually add the sugar. When the meringue begins to form

soft peaks, increase to a moderate beating speed.
- Beat another 5-8 minutes, until the meringue is thick, but still glossy, and forms firm peaks when the beaters are lifted.
- Adhere the parchment paper to the cookie sheet with dots of meringue.
- Spoon the meringue into a piping bag fitted with desired tip. Keep designs simple as these pieces are delicate and will shatter easily. Bake small pieces about 15 minutes and thicker pieces 15-20 minutes.

Nutrition Information

- Calories: 3.6
- Fiber: 0
- Total Carbohydrate: 0.1
- Cholesterol: 0
- Protein: 0.7
- Total Fat: 0
- Saturated Fat: 0
- Sodium: 11
- Sugar: 0.1

130. Swiss Mocha Coffee Mix

Serving: 4-6 serving(s) | Prep: 5mins | Ready in:

Ingredients

- 1/2 cup instant coffee
- 1 cup sugar
- 1 cup instant dry milk powder
- 1/4 cup powdered coffee creamer
- 1/4 cup unsweetened cocoa
- 1/4 cup vanilla instant pudding mix

Direction

- Measure all of the ingredients into a clean, dry bowl.
- Use a fork to combine everything evenly.
- Transfer this mixture into a resealable container.
- To Prepare: Measure 3 or 4 tablespoons of mixture in resealable container into a coffee mug.
- Fill coffee mug with hot water and stir to dissolve.

Nutrition Information

- Calories: 422.6
- Total Fat: 11.4
- Sugar: 65.6
- Total Carbohydrate: 72.9
- Cholesterol: 31
- Protein: 11.1
- Saturated Fat: 7.7
- Sodium: 134.5
- Fiber: 1.8

131. Swiss Vegetable Casserole

Serving: 6 serving(s) | Prep: 5mins | Ready in:

Ingredients

- 1 (10 3/4 ounce) can condensed cream of mushroom soup
- 1/3 cup sour cream
- 1/4 teaspoon ground black pepper
- 1 (16 ounce) bag frozen broccoli carrots cauliflower mix, thawed
- 1 (2 7/8 ounce) can French-fried onions (1 1/3 cups)
- 1/2 cup swiss cheese, shredded

Direction

- Mix first four ingredients together along with half the cheese.
- Bake at 350°F for 40 minute or until vegetables are tender. Stir.

- Top with remaining onions and cheese. Bake for 5 minute more.
- Note: You could use 1/2 cup shredded Cheddar cheese instead of Swiss cheese if you prefer the taste of cheddar.
- Note: I must admit that I usually make this with more cheese than the recipe calls for.

Nutrition Information

- Calories: 102.2
- Cholesterol: 14.9
- Protein: 3.5
- Sugar: 1.3
- Total Carbohydrate: 4.3
- Total Fat: 8
- Saturated Fat: 3.8
- Sodium: 383.7
- Fiber: 0

132. Swiss White Chocolate Coffee

Serving: 6 serving(s) | Prep: 12mins | Ready in:

Ingredients

- 5 ounces white chocolate, chopped
- 3 cups half-and-half
- 3 cups hot coffee
- 1 tablespoon brandy (or to taste)
- whipped cream
- 6 stemed maraschino cherries (to garnish)

Direction

- Heat the half and half and chocolate together in a saucepan until melted and smooth.
- Stir in coffee and brandy, serve with whipped cream and a cherry on top.

Nutrition Information

- Calories: 300.8
- Sodium: 73.5
- Fiber: 0.2
- Sugar: 16.1
- Total Carbohydrate: 21.3
- Protein: 5.1
- Total Fat: 21.5
- Saturated Fat: 13.2
- Cholesterol: 49.7

133. Tartiflette Alpine Melted Cheese, Bacon And Potato Gratin

Serving: 1 Tartiflette, 4 serving(s) | Prep: 15mins | Ready in:

Ingredients

- 1 1/2 kg potatoes
- 1 large onion, peeled and finely diced
- 200 g smoked lardons (8 ozs) or 200 g smoked streaky bacon, diced (8 ozs)
- 25 g butter (1 oz)
- 1/4 pint white wine (1 wine glass)
- 4 tablespoons creme fraiche or 4 tablespoons sour cream
- 1 garlic clove, peeled and cut in half
- sea salt
- fresh ground black pepper or fresh ground black pepper
- fresh ground black pepper
- 1 ripe reblochon cheese

Direction

- Preheat the oven to 200°C/400°F/gas mark 5.
- Bring a large pan of water to the boil and cook the potatoes whole, in their skins, for 15 minutes.
- Meanwhile, cook the onion and bacon in the butter in a heavy frying pan over a medium heat; they should sweat but not brown. When they are cooked, discard the fat and add the

glass of wine and the creme fraiche and mix well.

- Drain the potatoes and as soon as they are cool enough to handle peel them — the quicker the better. Slice thinly across.
- Choose an ovenproof earthenware dish and rub it well with the cut halves of garlic. Layer half the sliced potatoes across the base, season them with salt and freshly ground black pepper, then scatter over half the onion and bacon mixture.
- Cut the Reblochon cheese in half through the centre of the cheese, leaving you with a cut edge and a skin/rind edge, then lay one half of the cheese on top of the potato, bacon and onion mixture. Add the remaining bacon and onion mixture followed by the rest of the potatoes and more seasoning.
- Place the remaining half of cut Reblochon cheese skin/rind side up on top of the potatoes. Bake for 10 minutes, then reduce the heat to 180C/350'F/gas mark 4 for a further 20–25 minutes. The Reblochon should melt within its skin and the cheese drip down throughout the dish, while the potatoes will become crispy and golden brown.
- Tartiflette is a filling dish and all you really need to go with it is a mixed green salad, crusty French bread and a selection of pickles.

Nutrition Information

- Calories: 483.2
- Total Fat: 11
- Saturated Fat: 6.8
- Cholesterol: 33.9
- Protein: 8.5
- Sodium: 79.2
- Fiber: 8.9
- Sugar: 5.5
- Total Carbohydrate: 72.3

134. Three Cheese Fondue With Tomato Onion Chutney

Serving: 4-6 serving(s) | Prep: 72hours | Ready in:

Ingredients

- TOMATO ONION CHUTNEY
- 2 1/2 cups chopped onions
- 1 teaspoon mustard seeds
- 3 1/2 tablespoons unsalted butter
- 1 (14 ounce) can tomatoes, drained well in a colander
- 1 tablespoon red wine vinegar
- 1 tablespoon sugar
- 1/8 teaspoon ground allspice
- 2 tablespoons minced fresh parsley leaves
- THREE-CHEESE FONDUE WITH TOMATO ONION CHUTNEY
- 1/2 lb gruyere, grated coarse (about 2 1/2 cups)
- 1/2 lb emmenthaler cheese, grated coarse (about 2 1/2 cups)
- 1/2 lb doux de montagne cheese or 1/2 lb havarti cheese or 1/2 lb vacherin fribourgeois cheese, grated coarse (about 2 1/2 cups)
- 2 tablespoons cornstarch
- 1 clove garlic, halved
- 1 cup dry white wine
- 2 teaspoons fresh lemon juice
- 2 tablespoons calvados
- Accompaniments
- soft breadstick, with fennel seed
- assorted cooked vegetables, such as broccoli,cauliflower,carrots,and pearl onions
- cooked tortellini

Direction

- TOMATO ONION CHUTNEY: In a heavy skillet cook the onion and the mustard seeds in the butter over moderate heat until the onion begins to turn golden.
- Add the tomatoes, the vinegar, the sugar, and the allspice, cook the mixture, stirring and breaking up the tomatoes with a wooden spoon, until the chutney is very thick, and add the parsley and salt and pepper to taste.

- The chutney may be made 3 days in advance and kept covered and chilled.
- Makes about 2 cups THREE-CHEESE FONDUE WITH TOMATO ONION CHUTNEY: In a large bowl toss together well the cheese and the cornstarch.
- Rub the inside of a heavy saucepan with the garlic, leaving it in the pan, add the wine, 3/4 cup water, and the lemon juice, and boil the mixture for 1 minute.
- Stir in the cheese mixture gradually and bring the mixture to a simmer over moderate heat, stirring.
- Stir in the Calvados and simmer the mixture, stirring, for 2 minutes.
- Transfer the fondue to a fondue pot, swirl in the chutney, and set the fondue pot on its stand over a low flame.
- Serve the breadsticks, the potatoes, the vegetables, and the tortellini for dipping into the fondue.
- Stir the fondue often to keep it combined.

Nutrition Information

- Calories: 651.8
- Total Fat: 42.9
- Saturated Fat: 26
- Sugar: 10.9
- Protein: 30.5
- Sodium: 755.5
- Fiber: 3.1
- Total Carbohydrate: 27.2
- Cholesterol: 125.7

135. Traditional Swiss Fondue

Serving: 6 serving(s) | Prep: 15mins | Ready in:

Ingredients

- 2 cups dry white wine (such as Fendant)
- 1 tablespoon lemon juice
- 1 1/2 teaspoons Dijon mustard or 1 1/2 teaspoons dry English-style mustard
- 4 cups gruyere cheese, shredded (1 lb)
- 4 cups shredded Fontina cheese or 4 cups emmenthaler cheese or 4 cups monterey jack cheese
- 1 tablespoon arrowroot
- 2 ounces kirsch
- 1 pinch nutmeg
- serve with
- 1 lb French bread, cut into bite sized cubes or 1 lb red potatoes, cut in half boiled

Direction

- In fondue pot, heat wine, lemon juice and mustard to boiling; then reduce heat to low.
- Toss cheese with arrowroot and gradually add cheese mixture to wine mixture in pot, stirring constantly.
- When cheese is melted, stir in kirsch.
- Sprinkle with nutmeg, and serve with French bread or potatoes.

Nutrition Information

- Calories: 856
- Saturated Fat: 27.9
- Fiber: 2.4
- Sugar: 2.4
- Total Carbohydrate: 44.1
- Total Fat: 48
- Cholesterol: 162.7
- Protein: 46.7
- Sodium: 1296.3

136. Triple Double Trouble A.k.a. The Painkiller

Serving: 1 Mega Cocktail | Prep: 2mins | Ready in:

Ingredients

- 4 fluid ounces frozen vodka

- 4 fluid ounces Amaretto
- 4 fluid ounces Southern Comfort
- 1/2 fluid ounce chilled orange juice (actually a "splash") or 1/2 fluid ounce chilled pineapple juice (actually a "splash")

Direction

- Combine all above in a cocktail shaker.
- Shake, shake, shake.
- Pour into tall glass.
- Serve Straight up.
- Or on the rocks: Add a couple of ice cubes if they will fit (totally optional).
- Or as a frozen drink: Add several ice cubes into a Cuisinart and then add drink mixture and blend until it has the consistency of a frozen margarita.

Nutrition Information

- Calories: 591.9
- Fiber: 0
- Sugar: 1.3
- Cholesterol: 0
- Protein: 0.1
- Total Fat: 0
- Sodium: 2.4
- Saturated Fat: 0
- Total Carbohydrate: 1.6

---

137. White Asparagus In White Sauce

Serving: 4 serving(s) | Prep: 5mins | Ready in:

Ingredients

- 2 (14 1/2 ounce) cans white asparagus, drained reserving liquid
- 2 tablespoons margarine
- 2 tablespoons unbleached flour
- 1/2 cup asparagus water
- 1/2 cup milk
- 4 ounces cooked ham, cut into julienne strips
- 1/3 teaspoon nutmeg, freshly grated
- 1/4 teaspoon salt

Direction

- Drain asparagus spears, reserving 1/2 cup of the liquid.
- Heat margarine in a saucepan.
- Add flour; blend.
- Gradually pour in asparagus liquid and milk.
- Stir constantly over low heat until sauce thickens and bubbles.
- Add cooked ham and seasonings.
- Gently stir in asparagus spears; heat through but do not boil.
- Serve in preheated serving dish.

Nutrition Information

- Calories: 203.3
- Total Fat: 12.1
- Fiber: 4.5
- Sugar: 3.9
- Total Carbohydrate: 12.4
- Cholesterol: 30.9
- Saturated Fat: 3.7
- Sodium: 248.6
- Protein: 13.6

Chapter 5: Awesome Swiss Recipes

***

138. "swiss" Round Steak With Onion Gravy

Serving: 4-6 serving(s) | Prep: 30mins | Ready in:

Ingredients

- 1 1/2-2 lbs round steaks
- 1/2-1 cup flour
- salt
- pepper
- 2 -3 tablespoons oil
- 1 large onion, sliced
- 2 garlic cloves, crushed
- 2 -3 cups beef broth

Direction

- Cut round steak into 6 serving size pieces.
- On a cutting board, dredge pieces with flour, salt and pepper.
- Pound flour into the meat with a meat mallet.
- Turn pieces, dredge, and pound until they can't hold any more flour.
- (This can be a messy process, so be warned!).
- In a large non-stick skillet, heat oil and brown steak pieces on both sides.
- Place in a covered casserole.
- Add onions and garlic to the skillet.
- Sauté until onions are limp (5 minutes).
- Place onions and garlic over steak pieces in casserole dish.
- Add enough beef broth to barely cover meat.
- The flour from the meat will thicken the broth as it bakes and will make its own gravy.
- Bake at 300F for 2 hours or until fork-tender.
- Serve over noodles or mashed potatoes.

Nutrition Information

- Calories: 469.2
- Fiber: 1.1
- Total Carbohydrate: 16
- Cholesterol: 124.2
- Total Fat: 26.9
- Sugar: 1.6
- Protein: 38.7
- Saturated Fat: 8.8
- Sodium: 543.7

139. A Symphony Of French Chocolate Truffles

Serving: 36-40 Chocolate Truffles, 18-20 serving(s) | Prep: 24hours | Ready in:

Ingredients

- Basic truffle mixture
- 5 ounces very best quality 70% solids dark chocolate
- 5 fluid ounces thick double cream
- 1 ounce unsalted butter
- 2 tablespoons rum or 2 tablespoons brandy
- For the plain truffles
- 1 tablespoon cocoa powder
- For the ginger truffles
- 1 ounce preserved gingerroot, very finely chopped, plus some extra cut into small pieces
- For the toasted almond truffles
- 1 ounce flaked toasted almond, very finely chopped
- For the chocolate-coated truffles
- 2 ounces dark chocolate (at least 70% cocoa solids)
- 1/2 teaspoon peanut oil
- cocoa, for dusting
- paper, sweet cases for the chocolate-coated truffle
- 1 sheet baking parchment paper (silicone paper)
- For Coco dusted truffles
- 60% minimum cocoa powder

Direction

- For the basic truffle mixture, break the chocolate into squares and place it in the bowl of a food processor. Switch on and grind the chocolate until it looks granular, like sugar.
- Now place the cream, butter and rum or brandy in a small saucepan and bring these to simmering point. Then, with the motor switched on, pour the mixture through the feeder tube of the processor and continue to blend until you have a smooth, blended mixture.

- Next transfer the mixture, which will be very liquid at this stage, into a bowl, allow it to get quite cold, then cover it with cling film and refrigerate overnight. Don't worry: it will thicken up after several hours.
- Next day divide the mixture equally among four small bowls, and keep each one in the fridge until you need it. Then proceed with the following to make four different varieties. Make sure you have all the little paper cases opened out ready before your hands get all chocolatey!
- Plain Truffles:
- For these, you simply sift 1 level dessertspoon of cocoa powder on to a flat plate, then take heaped half teaspoons of the first batch of truffle mixture and either dust each one straight away all over, which gives the truffle a rough, rock-like appearance, or dust your hands in cocoa and roll each piece into a ball and then roll it in the cocoa powder if you like a smoother look. Place it immediately into a paper case. Obviously, the less handling the better as the warmth of your hands melts the chocolate.
- Ginger truffles:
- Mix the finely chopped ginger into the second batch of truffle mixture using a fork, then proceed as above, taking small pieces, rolling or not (as you wish), and dusting with cocoa powder before transferring each one to a paper case.
- Toasted almond truffles:
- Sprinkle the very finely chopped toasted almond flakes on a flat plate, take half a teaspoonful of the third batch of truffle mixture and roll it round in the nuts, pressing them to form an outer coating.
- Chocolate-coated truffles:
- For these you need to set the chocolate and oil in a bowl over some hot but not boiling water and allow it to melt until it becomes liquid, and then remove the pan from the heat.
- Spread some silicone paper on a flat surface and, dusting your hands with cocoa, roll each truffle into a little ball.
- Using two flat skewers, one to spike the truffle and one to manoeuvre it, dip each truffle in the chocolate so that it gets a thin coating and then quickly transfer it to the paper. If the chocolate begins to thicken, replace the pan on the heat so that it will liquefy again.
- Leave the coated truffles to set completely then, using a palette knife; quickly transfer them into their waiting paper cases.
- Cocoa Dusted Truffles:
- Simple and quick, I use 60% French Cocoa powder for an extra chocolate rush! Simply take each truffle and drop into a bowl of cocoa powder, and gently turn the truffles around to coat them.
- Now arrange all the truffles in a box or boxes and cover. Keep them refrigerated and eat within three days. Alternatively, truffles are ideal for freezing.

Nutrition Information

- Calories: 109.9
- Total Fat: 11.1
- Saturated Fat: 6.4
- Sodium: 6.1
- Fiber: 2.1
- Sugar: 0.2
- Total Carbohydrate: 4
- Cholesterol: 14.7
- Protein: 2

140. Appenzell Style Oat Soup

Serving: 4-6 serving(s) | Prep: 5mins | Ready in:

Ingredients

- 1 cup Appenzeller cheese, shredded
- 2 tablespoons butter
- 1 small onions or 1 small leek, chopped
- 6 tablespoons oatmeal
- 1 sprig parsley
- 4 cups hot meat stock

- 1 cup cream
- 1 bunch chives, chopped

Direction

- Fry onion in butter until golden.
- Add oatmeal and simmer for 2-3 minutes, stirring constantly.
- Add parsley and leek and allow to cook briefly.
- Add stock and simmer for a further 15-20 minutes.
- Lastly, enrich with cream and pour into soup plates or bowls.
- Sprinkle thickly with the grated Appenzeller cheese and diced chives; serve immediately.

Nutrition Information

- Calories: 260.7
- Saturated Fat: 15.3
- Fiber: 1.1
- Sugar: 0.9
- Total Fat: 24.7
- Sodium: 72.3
- Total Carbohydrate: 8.5
- Cholesterol: 81.6
- Protein: 2.5

141. Après Ski Holiday Hot Chocolate With Brandy And Cream

Serving: 4 Tall Mugs, 4 serving(s) | Prep: 5mins | Ready in:

Ingredients

- Hot Chocolate
- 1 liter whole milk
- 200 g 70% cocoa solids chocolate, broken into small pieces
- 2 tablespoons brown sugar
- 4 -5 tablespoons brandy
- 1 -2 teaspoon ground cinnamon, to taste
- To Decorate
- 6 tablespoons whipped cream
- 4 teaspoons cocoa powder or 4 teaspoons ground cinnamon
- cinnamon stick, for stirrers (optional)

Direction

- Gently boil the milk in a large heavy based saucepan, remove as boiling point is reached.
- Place chocolate in a small pan and add 2 tablespoons of the milk. Stir over a low heat until melted, then add the melted chocolate mixture into the remaining milk, stirring well.
- Add the sugar, cinnamon and brandy. Adjust to taste at this point.
- Serve the brandy hot chocolate in tall heatproof glasses or mugs, top with a dollop of whipped cream lightly dusted with cocoa powder or cinnamon.
- Serve with a cinnamon stick for a "stirrer"!
- Salut!

Nutrition Information

- Calories: 529.8
- Fiber: 10.5
- Cholesterol: 29.3
- Sugar: 21.2
- Total Carbohydrate: 37.7
- Protein: 16.3
- Total Fat: 40
- Saturated Fat: 24.4
- Sodium: 126.5

142. Bacon And Swiss Cheese Dip

Serving: 2 cups, 10 serving(s) | Prep: 5mins | Ready in:

Ingredients

- 8 ounces cream cheese

- 1/2 cup ranch salad dressing
- 4 ounces swiss cheese, shredded
- 2 tablespoons green onions, slices
- 8 bacon, slices crisp-cooked (drained and crumbled)
- 1/2 cup crushed buttery cracker

Direction

- In a small saucepan (or could use microwave), combine cream cheese, ranch dressing, Swiss cheese and green onion slices. Heat until cheese is melted; stirring constantly until smooth. Place in a small bowl.
- Sprinkle with bacon and crushed crackers. Serve with whole crackers.

Nutrition Information

- Calories: 221.8
- Total Fat: 20.7
- Total Carbohydrate: 4.1
- Cholesterol: 43.8
- Protein: 5.5
- Saturated Fat: 8.5
- Sodium: 302
- Fiber: 0.2
- Sugar: 1.4

143. Bavarian Pretzel Rolls

Serving: 12-16 rolls | Prep: 2hours | Ready in:

Ingredients

- 1 tablespoon yeast
- 1 1/2 cups warm water, 105 - 110 F
- 2 teaspoons honey (sugar, honey, or brown sugar, I recommend honey)
- 4 1/2 cups flour, sifted
- 2 teaspoons salt
- 4 tablespoons butter, melted
- 2 quarts water
- 1/2 cup baking soda
- salt (Pretzel or Kosher salt for sprinkling)

Direction

- In a mixer bowl, add yeast and 1 1/2 cups warm water and let stand for about 5 minutes until it foams and smells yeasty.
- Add sweetener, flour, salt, and melted butter. Mix with the dough hook until it forms a dough ball, about a couple minutes.
- Cover and let rise about 1 hour. Punch down and turn ball on a lightly floured counter.
- Roll dough into a "rope" and cut into the approximate sizes you want your rolls - about 12-16 rolls is reasonable. Shape into rolls. You can try pulling the dough balls inside out and pinching the edges together on the bottom to form a nice rounded top and a flattish bottom. Don't make it more difficult than it has to be; they taste good even if they don't look perfect!
- Put the rolls on a parchment lined cookie sheet or two (they won't rise much more). Cover and let rise another 30 minutes.
- Pre-heat oven to 425 °F.
- Heat 2 quarts of water to boiling.
- When water is boiling and rolls have risen, slowly pour baking soda into the water. Be careful! If you pour too quickly, the pot may boil over. Baking soda is a fine powder, providing plenty of nucleation points for steam bubbles to form, and it releases some gas when it contacts the water, to boot.
- Use a slotted spoon or spatula to east the rolls into the baking soda bath and poach for about 30 seconds on each side (the more time they poach the crustier, browner, and more authentic they'll be -- the less time in the bath the more like mall pretzels they'll be -- both are good, it's up to you).
- Use slotted spoon to remove from bath and place back on cookie sheets.
- While still damp, sprinkle with pretzel or kosher salt and score top with a knife in a plus (+) shape to allow the rolls to expand attractively while baking.
- Bake at 425 °F for about 15 minutes or until caramel brown. (More or less depending on

your oven and personal preference). Rotate cookie sheets top to bottom and rear to front midway during baking, if you desire.
- Serving suggestions:
- For breakfast: serve warm with Irish butter and strawberry preserves.
- For snack: smear with cheddar cheese spread
- For lunch/dinner: cut in half and top with thin sliced roast beef and smoked Gouda cheese; broil until cheese is brown and bubbly.
- Or just eat them plain!

Nutrition Information

- Calories: 211.3
- Cholesterol: 10.2
- Saturated Fat: 2.5
- Fiber: 1.5
- Sugar: 1.1
- Protein: 5.3
- Total Fat: 4.4
- Sodium: 2983.4
- Total Carbohydrate: 37.1

144. Birchermuesli

Serving: 4 serving(s) | Prep: 5mins | Ready in:

Ingredients

- 4 tablespoons oats
- 8 tablespoons water
- 4 tablespoons sweet evaporated milk or 4 tablespoons cream
- honey (use as less sugar as possible) or sugar, according to your own taste (use as less sugar as possible)
- 2 lemons, juice of
- 8 apples

Direction

- Put oat flakes, water, sweet evaporated milk and juice of lemon in a bowl.
- Wash apples, cut in pieces, remove core (do not remove skin!)
- Grind apples into the bowl and mix well.
- Add sugar and honey according to your own taste and mix well again.
- Serve immediately.
- Variations:
- You may use plain yogurt instead of water and evaporated milk. You may also add cream, half and half or milk according to your own taste.
- Take any kind of berries, oranges or other fruits instead of or in addition to the apples.
- You may add 2 to 3 tablespoons grind almonds and/or hazelnuts.

Nutrition Information

- Calories: 253.6
- Protein: 3.8
- Total Fat: 2.5
- Fiber: 9.8
- Total Carbohydrate: 60
- Cholesterol: 4.6
- Saturated Fat: 0.9
- Sodium: 21.6
- Sugar: 38.4

145. Buendner Spinach With Smoked Bacon

Serving: 4 serving(s) | Prep: 0S | Ready in:

Ingredients

- 4 ounces smoked bacon (Speck)
- 1 garlic clove
- 2 cups spinach, fresh
- salt, pepper, and nutmeg to taste

Direction

- Cook the thinly sliced bacon until transparent.

- Chop the garlic and saute it in the bacon fat. Saute the spinach with the bacon and garlic until just cooked.
- Season to taste with salt, pepper and nutmeg.

Nutrition Information

- Calories: 157.9
- Total Fat: 11.9
- Fiber: 0.3
- Cholesterol: 31.2
- Protein: 11
- Saturated Fat: 3.9
- Sodium: 666.9
- Sugar: 0.1
- Total Carbohydrate: 1.2

Nutrition Information

- Calories: 1365.5
- Saturated Fat: 0.3
- Sodium: 22
- Fiber: 35.6
- Total Carbohydrate: 226
- Protein: 14.9
- Sugar: 157.1
- Cholesterol: 7.5
- Total Fat: 51.4

146. Chocolate Fondu

Serving: 1 pot | Prep: 10mins | Ready in:

Ingredients

- 3/4-1 lb dark semi-sweet chocolate, 35% cocoa solids
- 1 pint strawberry
- 1 -2 banana
- 1 melon
- 2 kiwi fruits
- 1 -2 apple
- 1 -2 pear

Direction

- Using fondue pot, slowly melt chocolate.
- Arrange fruits cut up in bit size pieces (use your imagination on choices) on a tray or nice serving platter.
- Set melted chocolate on burner and let your guests help themselves, using fondue forks.
- Also put out some lady fingers or other nice simple cookies to dip.

147. Chocolate Mischief Goddess Heaven Milkshakes Of Choice

Serving: 4 serving(s) | Prep: 10mins | Ready in:

Ingredients

- Shake
- 4 cups premium quality chocolate ice cream
- 2 cups milk, less for thicker shakes
- 1 teaspoon vanilla extract
- 2 ounces chocolate syrup (optional)
- 2 ounces cream cheese, Petit suisse your favorite soft cream cheese (optional)
- 2 ounces jam, like Swizz apricot, black cherry, current, blackberry, raspberry, marmalade (optional)
- 2 ounces kirsch (liqueurs of choice) (optional)
- Toppings
- 1/4 cup sweetened whipped cream
- 1 tablespoon chocolate shavings, for garnish
- 4 cherries (optional)

Direction

- Using a blender, blend ice cream, milk, vanilla, and one or any of the optional shake ingredients together until smooth.
- You can add a handful of ice cubes if trying to keep the calories down.
- Top with whipped cream and a Swiss Lindt chocolate shavings.

- Topping with optional cherry.
- Make it a chocolate covered cherry. ;).
- Enjoy!

Nutrition Information

- Calories: 386.2
- Cholesterol: 64.8
- Protein: 9.4
- Saturated Fat: 12.9
- Fiber: 1.9
- Sodium: 165.6
- Sugar: 33.9
- Total Carbohydrate: 44.1
- Total Fat: 20.9

148. Chocolate Mousse With Raspberry Puree

Serving: 4 serving(s) | Prep: 25mins | Ready in:

Ingredients

- For the mousse
- 1 pint heavy cream
- 1/2 cup sugar
- 1/4 cup water
- 12 ounces white chocolate (optional) or 12 ounces bittersweet chocolate (optional) or 12 ounces semisweet chocolate, melted, divided use, cut into 1/4 inch chunks (optional)
- 1/2 cup egg white
- 1/2 teaspoon cream of tartar
- For the puree
- 1 1/2 cups raspberries
- 1/4 cup sugar

Direction

- Whip the heavy cream with a hand-held mixer or standing kitchen mixer for about 4 minutes, or until it forms whipped cream.
- Set aside.
- Mix a simple syrup by heating the water and sugar together in a small saucepan until boiling.
- Using an electric mixer, beat the egg whites and syrup together until eggs are stiff.
- Add cream of tartar and mix two more minutes.
- Blend in the melted chocolate, chocolate chunks and whipped cream.
- Chill for at least 2 hours.
- For the raspberry puree, cook the berries and sugar over medium heat for 4 minutes.
- Puree and cool.

Nutrition Information

- Calories: 596.4
- Total Fat: 44.4
- Saturated Fat: 27.4
- Sodium: 96.6
- Protein: 6.3
- Fiber: 3
- Sugar: 39.9
- Total Carbohydrate: 46.8
- Cholesterol: 163

149. Chocolate Orange Toppers

Serving: 4 serving(s) | Prep: 3hours30mins | Ready in:

Ingredients

- 1/4 liter milk
- 50 g chocolate (recipe specifies "with a hint of oranges")
- 3 eggs
- 2 egg yolks
- 30 g sugar
- 1 orange
- butter (for the moulds)
- SAUCE
- 50 g plain dark chocolate

- 1/8 liter cream

Direction

- Bring the milk to boiling point and remove from the hob. Break up the chocolate and dissolve in the milk. Briefly beat the eggs, the egg yolk and the sugar. Wash the orange in hot water, and dry. Grate half of the orange zest finely into the creamed egg mixture, followed by the hot chocolate milk. Preheat the oven to 160 °C. Boil the water.
- Butter 4 ovenproof timbale or soufflé moulds. Pour the mixture into the buttered oven-proof moulds. Cover with aluminum foil. Place inside an ovenproof dish. Pour boiling water into the dish up to two thirds the height of the moulds. Place in the centre of the oven to poach for 30-40 minutes (the time depends on the diameter of the moulds). Remove from the oven and allow to cool. Place in a cool place for at least 3 hours.
- Remove the remaining orange peel in strips. Blanch the strips in boiling water. Drain, then pour cold water onto the strips. Remove the rest of the orange peel to reveal the flesh, cut the fruit into tiny dice.
- For the sauce, just before serving, break up the plain chocolate. Dissolve it with the cream in a hot bain marie. Turn the toppers out onto a plate. Decorate with the chocolate sauce, the cubes of orange and the zests. Serve immediately.
- HINT. Add a decoration of chocolate curls: Place some melted Edelbitter plain chocolate onto a cold marble slab, roll it out smooth and, when dry, use a spatula to prise it from the board so that it curls into a little roll.

Nutrition Information

- Calories: 347.2
- Sodium: 90.7
- Fiber: 4.9
- Total Carbohydrate: 21.9
- Sugar: 11
- Cholesterol: 256.2
- Protein: 11.3
- Total Fat: 28
- Saturated Fat: 15.8

150. Chocolate Swiss Roll, Diabetic

Serving: 12 serving(s) | Prep: 20mins | Ready in:

Ingredients

- CAKE
- 4 eggs, separated
- 1/2 teaspoon cream of tartar
- 2 tablespoons splenda sugar substitute
- 3/4 cup skim milk
- 2 teaspoons vanilla flavoring
- 1/4 teaspoon almond flavoring
- 3/4 cup all-purpose flour
- 1/3 cup cocoa
- 3 tablespoons splenda sugar substitute
- 1 teaspoon baking powder
- 1/2 teaspoon baking soda
- 1/4 teaspoon salt
- WHIPPED FILLING
- 1 1/3 cups non-dairy coffee creamer, powder
- 2/3 cup nonfat milk (may need more, if so add slowly)
- 2 tablespoons Splenda sugar substitute (or to taste)
- 1/2 teaspoon vanilla flavoring
- 1/2 teaspoon other flavoring (brandy, almond, maple, etc.)

Direction

- MAKE FILLING:
- Chill small mixer bowl and beaters in freezer.
- Add creamer and milk; whip until stiff peaks form, scraping bowl occasionally.
- Add Splenda, flavorings and whip to mix. Refrigerate.
- CAKE:

- Spray jelly roll pan (15x10x1 inch) with Baker's Joy or grease well and lightly flour pan.
- Beat egg whites with cream of tartar at high speed until foamy. Add 2 tablespoons Splenda, beat until stiff peaks form; set aside.
- Beat yolks 5 minutes until thick and lemon colored. Blend in milk and flavoring; then add dry ingredients, mixing at low speed until moistened. Beat 2 minutes at medium, scraping sides occasionally.
- Pour yolk mixture over whites, carefully fold by hand until evenly blended. Pour into pan and bake 7 minutes until done. Set 1 minute; loosen around edges. Invert onto towel, roll with towel from narrow end, leaving open side on bottom. Cool completely on a rack.
- Unroll and spread cake with Whipped Frosting to within 1/2 inch of edges. Save some frosting for garnish. Roll cake with frosting, decorating top of roll with frosting and toasted almond pieces. Chill until serving time. Cut into 1/2 inch slices.

Nutrition Information

- Calories: 129.1
- Fiber: 0.7
- Sugar: 7.8
- Cholesterol: 62.6
- Protein: 4.8
- Total Fat: 4.6
- Saturated Fat: 1.1
- Sodium: 190.9
- Total Carbohydrate: 16.6

151. Creamy Swiss Chard Pasta

Serving: 4 serving(s) | Prep: 15mins | Ready in:

Ingredients

- 1 lb swiss chard
- 1 tablespoon olive oil
- 2 garlic cloves, smashed
- 1/4 cup onion, chopped
- 2 large tomatoes, chopped
- 1/2 cup fat free sour cream or 1/2 cup plain yogurt
- 1/2 cup 2% low-fat milk
- 1/4 cup parmesan cheese
- 8 ounces fettuccine pasta, cooked according to package
- salt and pepper

Direction

- Wash Swiss chard, cut into small pieces.
- Heat oil in large 2 quart saucepan over medium high heat, 1 to 2 minutes.
- Add Swiss chard, garlic and onion; cooking 1 to 2 minutes, stirring occasionally.
- Add tomatoes, sour cream, milk, parmesan cheese, cooked fettuccine, salt and pepper to taste; stir well.
- Serve warm.

Nutrition Information

- Calories: 314.9
- Saturated Fat: 2.4
- Sugar: 8
- Total Carbohydrate: 48
- Cholesterol: 53.8
- Protein: 14.6
- Total Fat: 8
- Sodium: 395.3
- Fiber: 3.1

152. Croutes Aux Champignons (Mushrooms On Toast)

Serving: 4 serving(s) | Prep: 10mins | Ready in:

Ingredients

- 1/4 cup onion, chopped

- 2 tablespoons butter
- 1 lb wild mushroom, sliced (chanterelles, cepes, or whatever you like)
- salt
- pepper
- 7 ounces dry white wine
- 4 ounces cream
- 4 slices bread, a hearty country bread is best
- 4 tablespoons grated parmesan cheese (or Sbrinz, if you can get it)

Direction

- Preheat broiler.
- Melt the butter in a large skillet. Add the onion, and cook until softened, but not brown. Add the mushrooms, season with salt and pepper to taste. Cover and cook over medium heat until the juices start to run. Uncover, and cook until the liquid evaporates.
- Add the wine, reduce by half. Add the cream, stir, and let simmer a few minutes, until thickened.
- Toast the bread, and place on a baking sheet. Top with the mushroom mixture and grated cheese.
- Place the toasts under the broiler, just until the top starts to brown. Serve immediately.

Nutrition Information

- Calories: 292.2
- Cholesterol: 51.4
- Total Fat: 17.2
- Sodium: 273.2
- Total Carbohydrate: 19.6
- Sugar: 4.3
- Protein: 8.2
- Saturated Fat: 10.3
- Fiber: 1.9

153. Crustless Bacon, Spinach Swiss Quiche Low Carb

Serving: 8 serving(s) | Prep: 20mins | Ready in:

Ingredients

- 1 lb bacon
- 1 large onion, chopped
- 2 tablespoons butter, divided
- 1 teaspoon olive oil
- 10 ounces frozen spinach, thawed
- 6 ounces swiss cheese, shredded
- 6 eggs
- 1/2 cup heavy whipping cream
- salt
- pepper

Direction

- On a foil lined pan, cook bacon in 350 degree F. oven until crisp.
- While bacon cooks, chop onion and shred cheese.
- Heat 1 tablespoon butter and 1 teaspoon oil in skillet over medium heat. Add chopped onion, and stir to coat.
- When onion turns glossy, add thawed spinach, and stir to mix. Heat about 5 minutes, then remove from heat to cool.
- Remove bacon from oven, and place on a paper-towel lined plate to drain.
- Stir together eggs, salt, pepper heavy whipping cream in a medium bowl.
- Add in cheese, onion/spinach mixture, and bacon. Stir thoroughly to mix.
- Butter a glass pie plate or quiche dish, pour mix in, and pat evenly with a fork.
- Bake in 350 degrees F. oven 25-30 minutes, or until a knife inserted in the center comes out clean.
- Let rest 5 minutes before cutting serving.
- I bet you can't eat just ONE slice!

Nutrition Information

- Calories: 494.8

- Total Fat: 44.2
- Saturated Fat: 18.8
- Fiber: 1.4
- Sugar: 1.5
- Protein: 19
- Sodium: 627.1
- Total Carbohydrate: 5.6
- Cholesterol: 225.7

154. Crustless Swiss Chard Quiche

Serving: 1 quiche, 8 serving(s) | Prep: 15mins | Ready in:

Ingredients

- 1 teaspoon olive oil
- 1/2 sweet onion
- 1/2 bunch swiss chard
- 2 1/2 cups shredded cheese
- 4 eggs
- 1 cup skim milk
- salt
- pepper

Direction

- Preheat oven to 375 degrees.
- Wash and dry Swiss chard. Cut off the very ends of the stems. Roughly chop (leaving stems intact) the chard.
- Add onion and Chard to the oil and sauté until stems are tender (do not overcook). Add salt pepper to taste.
- Meanwhile, grate 2.5 cups of cheese. Use whatever varieties you want/have. Be creative! I used Swiss, Cheddar, Parmesan, and Cotija.
- Wisk eggs. Add milk and cheese. Fold in the onion/chard mixture. Add salt pepper to taste, if necessary.
- Pour into a pie dish that has been sprayed with non-stick cooking spray.
- Bake for 35-45 minutes or until golden brown and no liquid seeps when you poke it with a knife.

Nutrition Information

- Calories: 177.5
- Total Fat: 11.7
- Saturated Fat: 6.3
- Sodium: 446.2
- Fiber: 0.5
- Sugar: 0.7
- Total Carbohydrate: 6.4
- Cholesterol: 116.2
- Protein: 11.8

155. Deviled Ham And Swiss Cheese Spread

Serving: 2 cups, 8 serving(s) | Prep: 2mins | Ready in:

Ingredients

- 8 ounces lean cooked ham, cubed
- 4 ounces swiss cheese, shredded (best quality)
- 3 tablespoons mayonnaise
- 1 tablespoon spicy brown mustard (Gulden's)
- 1 teaspoon sweet pickle relish

Direction

- Mix all ingredients in a food processor for 1-2 minutes until smooth.
- Serve with crackers or as a sandwich between 2 slices of bread. Makes about 2 cups.

Nutrition Information

- Calories: 154.9
- Total Fat: 10.9
- Saturated Fat: 4.6
- Sugar: 0.7
- Total Carbohydrate: 2.4
- Cholesterol: 41.1

- Protein: 11.6
- Sodium: 109.8
- Fiber: 0.1

156. Fluffy Omelette With Ham, Spinach And Swiss Cheese

Serving: 1 serving(s) | Prep: 5mins | Ready in:

Ingredients

- 2 eggs, separated
- 1 tablespoon milk
- 1/2 cup baby spinach leaves
- 2 slices shaved ham, torn roughly
- 1/4 cup grated lowfat swiss cheese

Direction

- Place the egg yolks in a bowl with the milk and combine. In a separate bowl, whisk the egg whites to medium soft peaks. Gently fold into the egg yolk mixture. Set aside (do not allow to sit for too long).
- Spray a small non-stick frying pan with oil spray and place over medium heat. Add the baby spinach and cook for 1-2 minutes or until wilted. Remove from pan and wipe pan clean. Spray pan again and return to the heat.
- Pour in the egg mixture and cook for 2-3 minutes or until surface is nearly firm. Place the ham, spinach and cheese over half the omelette, then fold over the other side to enclose the filling. Serve immediately. Repeat ingredients and method for additional omelettes.
- Source.

Nutrition Information

- Calories: 213.3
- Total Fat: 11.8
- Saturated Fat: 4.6

- Sodium: 247.1
- Sugar: 0.9
- Cholesterol: 385.7
- Fiber: 0.3
- Total Carbohydrate: 3.1
- Protein: 22.9

157. Grilled Turkey And Swiss Panini Sandwich

Serving: 1 sandwich, 1 serving(s) | Prep: 5mins | Ready in:

Ingredients

- 2 slices sourdough bread
- 1 -2 tablespoon apricot jam
- 4 ounces sliced turkey breast
- 1 slice sweet onion
- 1/2 tablespoon chopped roasted red pepper (from a jar)
- 2 slices swiss cheese
- nonstick cooking spray (olive oil or butter flavored)

Direction

- Preheat skillet or griddle to medium high and spray with nonstick spray.
- Spread jam on one piece of bread.
- On other piece of bread, place turkey, onion slice, roasted red peppers and Swiss cheese.
- Place bread spread with jam on top of other side of sandwich and put on griddle.
- Cover with a deep pot lid and cook a minute or so (until lightly browned).
- Remove lid, flip sandwich carefully and cook other side about a minute or so (until lightly browned).
- If sandwich browns before cheese melts, put it in the microwave for 15 seconds or so.

Nutrition Information

- Calories: 794.5
- Cholesterol: 125.2
- Protein: 51.4
- Total Fat: 27.4
- Saturated Fat: 12.9
- Sodium: 1020.9
- Sugar: 8.8
- Total Carbohydrate: 83.4
- Fiber: 4.1

158. Ham And Cheese Rösti

Serving: 4-6 serving(s) | Prep: 25mins | Ready in:

Ingredients

- 1 large egg
- 1 cup ham, diced (about 5 ounces)
- 1 cup low-fat cheese, shredded
- 1 shallot, minced
- 1/4 teaspoon dried rosemary
- 1/2 teaspoon ground pepper
- 1/4 teaspoon salt
- 4 cups frozen hash brown potatoes
- 2 teaspoons extra virgin olive oil, divided

Direction

- Beat egg in a large bowl. Stir in ham, 1/2 cup cheese, shallot, rosemary, pepper, and salt. Add frozen potatoes and stir to combine.
- Heat 1 teaspoon oil in a large non-stick skillet over medium heat.
- When oil is hot (test with a drop of water; oil should sputter, but should not be smoking), pat potato mixture into an even round in the pan. Cover and cook until browned and crispy on the bottom, 5 to 7 minutes.
- Remove pan from heat.
- Place a rimless baking sheet on top. Wearing oven mitts, grasp the pan and baking sheet together and carefully invert, unmolding the rosti onto the baking sheet.
- Wipe out any browned bits from the skillet.
- Return it to the heat and add the remaining oil. Slide rosti back into the pan, browned side up.
- Top with remaining 1/2 cup cheese, cover and cook the second side until crispy and browned, 4 to 6 minutes.
- Slide onto a platter and let stand 5 minutes.
- Cut into wedges and serve.

Nutrition Information

- Calories: 272.1
- Total Fat: 7.1
- Saturated Fat: 2.5
- Fiber: 3
- Sugar: 0.3
- Cholesterol: 59.8
- Sodium: 411.8
- Total Carbohydrate: 39
- Protein: 14.1

159. Ham And Swiss Loaded Baked Potatoes

Serving: 4 serving(s) | Prep: 10mins | Ready in:

Ingredients

- 4 baking potatoes (about 1 1/2 pounds)
- 1 cup diced ham (about 6 ounces)
- 1 cup shredded swiss cheese, divided
- 1/2 cup thinly sliced green onion, divided
- 1/2 cup nonfat sour cream
- 1/4 teaspoon fresh ground black pepper

Direction

- Pierce potatoes with a fork; arrange in a circle on paper towels in microwave oven.
- Microwave at high 16 minutes or until done, rearranging potatoes after 8 minutes. Let stand 5 minutes.
- Preheat broiler.

- Cut each potato in half lengthwise; scoop out pulp, leaving a 1/4-inch-thick shell. Combine potato pulp, ham, 1/2 cup cheese, 1/3 cup green onions, sour cream, and pepper.
- Spoon the potato mixture into shells. Combine 1/2 cup cheese and remaining green onions, and sprinkle over potatoes. Place potatoes on a baking sheet; broil 4 minutes or until golden.

Nutrition Information

- Calories: 305.8
- Sodium: 613
- Fiber: 2.8
- Sugar: 4.1
- Total Carbohydrate: 34.7
- Cholesterol: 45.9
- Total Fat: 10.1
- Protein: 19.4
- Saturated Fat: 5.8

160. Karen's Swiss Steak (Stove Top, Crock Pot Or Oven)

Serving: 6 serving(s) | Prep: 30mins | Ready in:

Ingredients

- 1 1/2 lbs beef round steak, cut 3/4 inch thick
- 3 tablespoons flour
- 1 teaspoon salt
- 1 teaspoon dry mustard
- 1/4 teaspoon pepper
- 3 teaspoons garlic powder
- 2 teaspoons shortening
- 1 (16 ounce) can tomatoes
- 1 small onion, sliced
- 1 stalk celery, sliced
- 2 medium carrots, sliced
- 1 tablespoon Worcestershire sauce
- 1/4 cup red wine
- 1/4 cup water
- hot cooked noodles
- mashed potatoes or hot cooked rice

Direction

- Cut meat into 6 serving pieces.
- Combine flour, salt, mustard, pepper, and garlic powder.
- Put 2 T. of the flour mixture into the meat.
- Brown the meat in the shortening on both sides.
- Drain off excess fat.
- Add undrained tomatoes, onion, celery, carrots, Worcestershire sauce and cooking wine.
- Cover and simmer for 1 1/4 hours or until meat is tender.
- Remove meat to a serving platter and keep warm.
- Combine 1/4 water and the remaining flour mixture.
- Stir into tomato mixture until thick and bubbly.
- Pass with meat.
- Serve meat and sauce with hot cooked noodles or rice.
- Crock pot directions:
- Prepare Swiss steak as above except cut meat to fit your crock pot.
- After browning meat, transfer to crock pot.
- Stir remaining flour into pan drippings in the skillet.
- Stir in the remaining ingredients and cook until thick and bubbly.
- Pour over meat in the crock pot.
- Cook on low for 8 to 10 hours.
- Serve with hot cooked noodles or rice.
- Oven directions:
- Place meat in a baking dish.
- Cover with thickened drippings and veggies as above.
- Bake, uncovered, in a 350 degree oven for 1 hour and 20 minutes.
- Serve with hot noodles or rice.

Nutrition Information

- Calories: 72.2
- Saturated Fat: 0.4
- Sugar: 4
- Cholesterol: 0
- Total Fat: 1.8
- Sodium: 440.8
- Fiber: 2.1
- Total Carbohydrate: 11.3
- Protein: 1.8

161. Kings Hawaiian Ham Swiss Slider

Serving: 24 sandwiches, 12 serving(s) | Prep: 10mins | Ready in:

Ingredients

- 24 slices deli honey-roasted ham
- 6 slices swiss cheese
- 1/3 cup mayonnaise
- 1 tablespoon poppy seed
- 1 1/2 tablespoons Dijon mustard
- 1/2 cup butter, melted
- 1 tablespoon onion powder
- 1/2 teaspoon Worcestershire sauce
- 2 (12 count) packagesking's original hawaiian rolls

Direction

- Step 1.
- Spread mayo onto 1 side of roll. Place a slice or two of ham and slice of Swiss cheese in roll. Replace the top of the rolls and bunch them closely together into a baking dish.
- Step 2.
- In a medium bowl, whisk together poppy seeds, Dijon mustard, melted butter, onion powder and Worcestershire sauce.
- Step 3.
- Pour sauce over the rolls, just covering the tops. Cover with foil and let sit for 10 minutes.
- Step 4.
- Bake at 350 degrees for 10 minutes or until cheese is melted. Uncover and cook for additional 2 minutes until tops are slightly browned and crisp. Serve warm.

Nutrition Information

- Calories: 222.9
- Total Fat: 15.5
- Saturated Fat: 8.4
- Sugar: 0.7
- Cholesterol: 47.4
- Protein: 14.3
- Sodium: 675.3
- Fiber: 0.3
- Total Carbohydrate: 7.2

162. Lighter Grilled Swiss, Ham And Asparagus Sannie

Serving: 1 sandwich | Prep: 8mins | Ready in:

Ingredients

- 2 slices whole grain bread
- 2 ounces lean ham (deli or baked, can use more if you like)
- 2 slices fat-free swiss cheese
- 6 steamed asparagus spears, bottom ends trimmed to fit the bread (leftover is fine, use more or less as you choose)
- 1 1/2 teaspoons healthy balance margarine, divided

Direction

- Use 3/4 tsp margarine on one slice of bread and lay it in a cool skillet naked side up.
- Place 1 slice of the cheese on the bread.
- Top that with the ham.
- Layer on the asparagus.
- Top with the second cheese slice.
- Spread the remaining 3/4 tsp of margarine and place it on the sandwich.

- Turn on the heat and grill to your liking, flip it and grill the other side.
- Serve hot and enjoy.

Nutrition Information

- Calories: 285.8
- Total Fat: 10.5
- Sodium: 985.9
- Sugar: 4.3
- Total Carbohydrate: 27.2
- Saturated Fat: 2.5
- Fiber: 5.6
- Cholesterol: 17
- Protein: 21.4

super grainy type that may not represent the typical grain. Thank you Paula and Amis for the helpful feedback.

Nutrition Information

- Calories: 43.5
- Total Fat: 0.5
- Saturated Fat: 0.1
- Sodium: 1
- Fiber: 1.2
- Sugar: 2.9
- Total Carbohydrate: 8.8
- Cholesterol: 0
- Protein: 1.5

163. Low Fat Bircher Muesli

Serving: 3 cups, 24 serving(s) | Prep: 5mins | Ready in:

Ingredients

- 1/3 cup wheat germ
- 1 1/2 cups quick-cooking rolled oats
- 1/2 cup currants or 1/2 cup raisins
- 1/4 cup dried apricot, finely chopped
- 1/4 cup dried cranberries, chopped
- 1/4 cup barley malt or 1/4 cup brown sugar or 1/4 cup honey
- 1/4 teaspoon cinnamon

Direction

- Combine all ingredients together and store in an air tight container.
- For breakfast combine 1/4 cup of the muesli mix with 1/4 cup of water and let soak for 30 minutes. Serve with 1 cup of yogurt and chopped fruit. Diced apples strawberries, bananas and blueberries all work well.
- 9/14 update: After reading the reviewer comments, I'm changing the directions to a 1:1 ratio of muesli and water. While the 2:1 worked well for me, my oatmeal is an organic

164. Lumumba (Swiss Hot Chocolate With Peppercorns)

Serving: 4 serving(s) | Prep: 10mins | Ready in:

Ingredients

- 7/8 liter milk
- 50 g cocoa powder
- 50 g sugar
- 100 g extra dark chocolate (72 % cocoa)
- 1/8 liter rum
- pepper (three color peppercorns, freshly ground)
- chocolate, to decorate

Direction

- Bring the milk, cocoa powder and sugar to the boil, stirring all the while. Remove from the heat. Break up the chocolate. Dissolve it in the hot milk. Bring back to the boil, still stirring all the time. Pour the rum into the liquid. Add pepper to taste. Pour into heat-resistant glasses, dust with grated chocolate and serve immediately.
- HINT. If you wish, you can serve with semi-whipped cream. Place a spoon in the glass so

that it does not shatter when you pour in the hot liquid. It dissipates the heat.

Nutrition Information

- Calories: 277.4
- Sugar: 12.7
- Total Carbohydrate: 30.5
- Cholesterol: 31.9
- Protein: 10
- Total Fat: 10.1
- Sodium: 114.6
- Fiber: 4.3
- Saturated Fat: 6.2

165. Mushroom Swiss Veggie Burger

Serving: 1 burger, 1 serving(s) | Prep: 2mins | Ready in:

Ingredients

- 1 hamburger bun
- 1 portabella mushrooms (sauteed) or 1 mushroom-based veggie burger
- 1 slice swiss cheese
- 2 tablespoons barbecue sauce
- 1 tablespoon guacamole
- 2 slices fresh tomatoes
- iceberg lettuce

Direction

- Slather the top of the bun with guacamole, the bottom with BBQ.
- Add the mushroom/patty to the bun and top with Swiss, tomato, and lettuce. Enjoy!

Nutrition Information

- Calories: 277.9
- Saturated Fat: 5.6
- Total Carbohydrate: 32.4
- Cholesterol: 25.8
- Total Fat: 10.4
- Sodium: 511.3
- Fiber: 3
- Sugar: 6.8
- Protein: 14.6

166. Omelette (Pancakes/Crepes)

Serving: 10 crepes (approx), 3-4 serving(s) | Prep: 45mins | Ready in:

Ingredients

- 1 1/2 cups plain flour
- 1/2 cup self raising flour
- 2 eggs
- 1 1/2 cups water, mixed with
- 1 1/2 cups milk
- 2 teaspoons oil (flavourless, like sunflower)
- 1 pinch salt

Direction

- Sift flours (you don't have to but it makes them a bit lighter) into a bowl or wide jug.
- Add lightly beaten eggs and half the milk-water.
- Whisk with an electric whisk (or with beaters) until mixed, add the remaining milk-water.
- Whisk some more, for about 1 minute.
- Add oil and salt, whisk for 1 more minute until smooth and frothy.
- Refrigerate for 1/2 hour.
- Take out of the fridge and lightly whisk again, check consistency- it may need a little extra liquid at this stage but you probably won't be able to tell until you start making them.
- Spray a nonstick pan with oil and heat it up (not too hot!).
- Lift the pan off the heat. Ladle or pour a small amount of omelette mix into the pan. Rotate the pan so the omelette mix covers the bottom of the pan thinly and is even.

- Put the pan back on the heat and cook the underside until it is browned.
- Flip.
- Cook until ready.
- Remove the omelette from the pan and put on a plate, cover with another plate to keep them warm. Whilst you are making the others you can keep them like this in a warm oven. Don't worry if they look a little stiff, once they are stored like this (with the plate on top), the steam will soften them so that they roll nicely when you fill them.

Nutrition Information

- Calories: 455.6
- Sodium: 164
- Sugar: 0.3
- Total Carbohydrate: 69.5
- Cholesterol: 141.1
- Total Fat: 11.4
- Saturated Fat: 4.3
- Fiber: 2.2
- Protein: 16.8

167. Pommes De Terre Au Lard Or Speckkartoffeln (Bacon Potatoes)

Serving: 4-6 serving(s) | Prep: 10mins | Ready in:

Ingredients

- 2 lbs potatoes, peeled and cut into small cubes
- 8 ounces smoked bacon, cut into 1/4 inch strips
- salt freshly ground black pepper, to taste

Direction

- Heat a large frying pan over medium-high heat. Add potatoes and bacon, stirring frequently until potatoes are golden yellow and cooked through, about 20 minutes.
- Season with salt and pepper.
- Finally, remove the potatoes and bacon from the pan. Place them on a plate lined with paper towels to soak up some of the fat.
- These beautiful country potatoes go well with sausages (Vaud sausage) and sauerkraut.

Nutrition Information

- Calories: 481.5
- Sodium: 1323.4
- Sugar: 1.8
- Cholesterol: 62.4
- Protein: 25.6
- Total Fat: 23.9
- Saturated Fat: 7.8
- Fiber: 5
- Total Carbohydrate: 40.5

168. Saint Moritz Martini

Serving: 1 serving(s) | Prep: 2mins | Ready in:

Ingredients

- 2 fluid ounces raspberry liqueur
- 1 1/2 fluid ounces heavy cream
- 1 1/2 fluid ounces milk
- ice

Direction

- Add ingredients to a shaker filled with ice.
- Shake strain into 5 ounce martini glass.

Nutrition Information

- Calories: 183.5
- Sodium: 39.4
- Fiber: 0
- Sugar: 0.1
- Total Carbohydrate: 3.4
- Total Fat: 18.2
- Saturated Fat: 11.3

- Protein: 2.4
- Cholesterol: 67.6

169. Sautéed Swiss Chard With Garlic

Serving: 4 serving(s) | Prep: 5mins | Ready in:

Ingredients

- 500 g swiss chard
- 3 tablespoons extra virgin olive oil
- 1 fresh chili, roughly chopped
- 2 garlic cloves, roughly broken
- 1/2 lemon, juice only

Direction

- 1. Take the Swiss chard and separate the white stalks from the green leaves using a sharp knife. Chop both parts roughly into bite-size pieces, keeping the leaves separate from the stalks. Cook the stalks in plenty of boiling salted water for 5 minutes or until cooked through. Drain.
- 2. In a large frying pan, heat the olive oil over a moderate heat. Add the chilli and garlic, and season with black pepper.
- 3. Stir in the leaves, cover the pan and let them wilt for 5 minutes. Stir and cook uncovered for a further 5 minutes to reduce the juices in the pan.
- 4. Add the stalks and a little more olive oil if necessary. Taste and adjust seasoning and squeeze over a little lemon juice.

Nutrition Information

- Calories: 117.6
- Sodium: 266.9
- Fiber: 2.2
- Cholesterol: 0
- Protein: 2.4
- Total Fat: 10.4

- Saturated Fat: 1.4
- Sugar: 1.6
- Total Carbohydrate: 5.8

170. Skiers Swiss Cereal (Rainy Day Breakfast)

Serving: 1/2 cup, 4 serving(s) | Prep: 10mins | Ready in:

Ingredients

- 1 cup rolled oats
- 1 teaspoon orange zest, very finely chopped
- 1/2 teaspoon cinnamon
- 2 tablespoons dried tart cherries
- 2 cups skim milk, i use half and half
- brown sugar
- cream or butter or milk

Direction

- The night before, combine the oats, zest, cinnamon, and cherries in a glass bowl. Stir well, then stir in the milk. Cover with plastic wrap and refrigerate.
- In the morning, place the mixture in a medium-sized saucepan and bring it to a simmer.
- Lower the heat and cook, stirring frequently, for 4 to 6 minutes, or until the oats are tender and the mixture is thick.
- Serve immediately, either as it is or with brown sugar or granulated sugar, and cream, butter, or milk.

Nutrition Information

- Calories: 130.8
- Saturated Fat: 0.4
- Sodium: 74
- Sugar: 0.6
- Total Fat: 1.6
- Fiber: 2.4
- Total Carbohydrate: 21.5

- Cholesterol: 2.5
- Protein: 7.6

171. Spargel White Asparagus With Easy Hollandaise Sauce

Serving: 4-6 serving(s) | Prep: 10mins | Ready in:

Ingredients

- 3 tablespoons extra virgin olive oil (or unsalted butter)
- 2 lbs white asparagus, washed and trimmed
- 1/4 teaspoon finely chopped fresh lemon zest
- 2 -3 teaspoons fresh squeezed lemon juice
- 1/2 teaspoon kosher salt
- 1/4 teaspoon white pepper (optional)
- fresh snipped parsley, optional to serve
- fresh small fresh edible flower, optional to garnish (such as violets or Johnny jump-ups)
- Easy Hollandaise Sauce
- 1/2 cup butter (1 stick)
- 4 large egg yolks
- 1/2 cup heavy cream (or whipping cream)
- 2 tablespoons lemon juice (to taste)
- 1/4 teaspoon sugar
- 1/2 teaspoon Dijon mustard

Direction

- Warm the olive oil or butter in a large saucepan over medium heat. Add the peeled and trimmed asparagus, lemon zest, and salt pepper; stir to combine.
- Cover and cook until tender-crisp, about 5 minutes, stirring occasionally. Do not overcook.
- Arrange on serving platter and squeeze with fresh lemon juice.
- Prepare the Hollandaise Sauce: Cut the butter into four pieces and place in a 1-quart glass measure or bowl. Microwave, covered with a paper towel, on high, until almost melted (about 45 seconds to 1 minute).
- Remove butter from the microwave and stir until completely melted.
- Separate eggs, placing the yolks in a small bowl and setting the whites aside for another purpose. Beat the yolks well with a whisk or fork, then add to the butter and stir well.
- Add cream, lemon juice, and sugar to egg mixture and stir well. Microwave mixture, uncovered, on high, until just slightly thick, about 1 to 2 minutes, stopping every 20 seconds to stir with a fork. Remove sauce from microwave and stir in the mustard.
- Pour warm sauce over the cooked white asparagus and serve at once. Garnish with fresh snipped parsley or fresh small edible flowers such as violets or Johnny jump-ups, if desired.
- NOTE: Sauce may be kept warm for up to 2 hours in an insulated container. Or cool the sauce to room temperature and refrigerate it in a covered microwave safe container for up to 24 hours. To re-warm, cover container with plastic wrap, pierce wrap with a knife to vent, and microwave on 50 percent power until heated through, about 2-3 minutes, stopping to stir halfway through. Do not allow sauce to boil.

Nutrition Information

- Calories: 499.4
- Saturated Fat: 24.6
- Sodium: 452
- Total Carbohydrate: 11.3
- Protein: 8.6
- Total Fat: 49
- Fiber: 4.8
- Sugar: 4.9
- Cholesterol: 286.2

172. Spicy Swiss Chard Or Spinach

Serving: 2-3 | Prep: 5mins | Ready in:

Ingredients

- 2 tablespoons extra virgin olive oil
- 1 pinch red pepper flakes
- 2 garlic cloves, minced
- 1 bunch swiss chard, stems removed and leaves chopped into thin strips (or 2 bunches spinach)
- splash white wine (or wine vinegar)
- 1 tablespoon sugar
- salt

Direction

- In a large skillet over high heat, add oil, red pepper flakes and garlic and toast the garlic until golden brown(watch carefully, don't let it burn!).
- Add the chard or spinach and toss quickly.
- Stir in a splash of white wine.
- Cook and toss until liquid evaporates and greens are wilted.
- Add the sugar, season with salt and serve. Enjoy!

Nutrition Information

- Calories: 185.4
- Saturated Fat: 1.9
- Sodium: 409.9
- Fiber: 3.2
- Sugar: 8.4
- Total Carbohydrate: 14.6
- Cholesterol: 0
- Total Fat: 13.9
- Protein: 3.7

173. St. Moritz Cocktail

Serving: 1 serving(s) | Prep: 2mins | Ready in:

Ingredients

- 3/4 ounce raspberry liqueur (actually calls for black raspberry liqueur)
- 3/4 ounce cream

Direction

- Grab a shot glass and add 3/4 oz. of Black Raspberry Liqueur.
- Next, carefully pour 3/4 oz. of Cream over the back of a bar spoon to create a second layer.

Nutrition Information

- Calories: 62.6
- Total Fat: 6.6
- Saturated Fat: 4.1
- Sodium: 7.3
- Sugar: 0
- Total Carbohydrate: 0.6
- Fiber: 0
- Cholesterol: 23.8
- Protein: 0.5

174. Steamed Fish With Sour Cream Sauce

Serving: 4 serving(s) | Prep: 5mins | Ready in:

Ingredients

- 6 fish fillets (flounder, sole, perch, etc.)
- salt
- pepper
- 3 tablespoons flour
- 1/4 cup minced parsley
- 1/2 cup nonfat sour cream
- 1 cup chicken broth
- 2 tablespoons fresh lemon juice

Direction

- Sprinkle fish with salt. Heavily butter a skillet that is presentable at the table. Place the fillets in it side-by-side.
- Sprinkle with the flour and parsley. Spoon the sour cream in a thin layer over the fish. Pour in the chicken broth.
- Cook, uncovered over low heat, without turning, until the fish is flaky. Sprinkle the lemon juice over the fish.
- Place the skillet under the broiler. Broil until barely browned. Serve from the skillet.

Nutrition Information

- Calories: 346.7
- Saturated Fat: 0.8
- Sodium: 422.6
- Total Carbohydrate: 10.3
- Total Fat: 3.2
- Fiber: 0.3
- Sugar: 2.7
- Cholesterol: 151.4
- Protein: 65.1

175. Swiss Breakfast Parfait

Serving: 4 serving(s) | Prep: 10mins | Ready in:

Ingredients

- 1 cup old fashioned oats, uncooked
- 16 ounces vanilla yogurt
- 2 tablespoons sliced almonds
- 8 ounces crushed pineapple in juice, undrained
- 2 cups fresh strawberries or 2 cups blueberries
- sliced almonds, garnish

Direction

- In medium bowl, combine oats, yogurt, pineapple, and almonds. Mix well.
- Cover, refrigerate overnight or up to 3 days.
- To serve, layer oat mixture and berries in parfait glasses.
- Garnish with additional sliced almonds.

Nutrition Information

- Calories: 220.1
- Total Carbohydrate: 34.1
- Cholesterol: 14.9
- Sodium: 55.1
- Fiber: 4.3
- Sugar: 17.4
- Protein: 8
- Total Fat: 6.7
- Saturated Fat: 2.7

176. Swiss Cheese Bacon Smoked Almond Dip

Serving: 6 serving(s) | Prep: 10mins | Ready in:

Ingredients

- 10 slices bacon
- 8 ounces cream cheese, Softened
- 1/2 cup mayonnaise
- 2 teaspoons dijon-style mustard
- 1 1/2 cups swiss cheese, Shredded
- 4 green onions, Chopped
- 1/2 cup smoked almonds, Chopped

Direction

- Fry the bacon. Let drain and crumble.
- Mix all ingredients. Bake in 350 degree preheated oven for about 15 minutes; until golden and bubbly. Top with some crushed almonds.
- For a twist, put the cold dip in pre-packaged phyllo cups and bake for about 15 minutes.

Nutrition Information

- Calories: 364.8

- Total Fat: 32.5
- Saturated Fat: 14.6
- Fiber: 1.5
- Sugar: 2.4
- Sodium: 286.4
- Total Carbohydrate: 6.2
- Cholesterol: 75.6
- Protein: 13.7

177. Swiss Fondue Bread

Serving: 6 serving(s) | Prep: 10mins | Ready in:

Ingredients

- 1/3 cup mayonnaise
- 1/4 cup dry white wine
- 2 tablespoons scallions, rings
- 2 tablespoons Dijon mustard
- 2 cups shredded swiss cheese
- 1 loaf French bread (about 1 lb.) or 1 loaf Italian bread, cut in half lengthwise (about 1 lb.)

Direction

- Preheat the oven to broil.
- In medium bowl, combine mayonnaise, wine, scallion and mustard and mix well. Stir in the Swiss cheese.
- Place the 2 halves of bread, cut side up, under the broiler and toast lightly. Remove from oven and spread the cheese mixture evenly over each half. Return to the oven for 3-5 minutes or until the cheese is brown and bubbly. Slice bread and serve.

Nutrition Information

- Calories: 692.9
- Protein: 30.1
- Saturated Fat: 7.9
- Sodium: 1094.9
- Sugar: 5.9
- Total Carbohydrate: 102
- Cholesterol: 36.5
- Total Fat: 17.7
- Fiber: 4.3

178. Swiss Muesli

Serving: 2 serving(s) | Prep: 10mins | Ready in:

Ingredients

- 1 medium apple
- 1/2 cup thick low-fat plain yogurt
- 2 tablespoons chopped almonds
- 1 cup rolled oats
- 1/2 teaspoon cinnamon, if desired

Direction

- Grate apple, including skin.
- Put into mixing bowl.
- Add yoghurt and mix well.
- Stir in nuts, oats and cinnamon (if using).
- Combine well.
- Serve.
- Nice served with fresh fruit and nuts.

Nutrition Information

- Calories: 304.8
- Fiber: 6.9
- Sugar: 19.8
- Protein: 11.2
- Sodium: 66
- Total Carbohydrate: 50.4
- Cholesterol: 2.5
- Total Fat: 7.7
- Saturated Fat: 1.2

179. Swiss Spaetzle (Very Easy Homemade Noodle)

Serving: 4-6 serving(s) | Prep: 20mins | Ready in:

Ingredients

- 3 cups flour
- 3 eggs
- 1/2 cup milk
- 3/4 cup water
- 1 teaspoon salt

Direction

- Heat water in a big pot for cooking.
- Meanwhile mix flour, eggs, milk, water and salt together with a blender.
- Let rest 5 to 10 minutes and mix briefly.
- Add salt to the boiling water.
- Add the dough directly into the boiling water quickly using a holed colander or a spaetzle maker.
- When the spaetzle float, they are ready; it takes about 2 or 3 minutes.
- You can prepare colorful spaetzle if you add to the dough:
- For red: some tomato concentrate.
- For yellow: 1 teaspoon turmeric powder.
- For green: 1/2 cup mashed spinach.
- For orange: 1 cup of mashed cooked squash or carrots; reduce the water to about 1/2 cup.
- And so on….

Nutrition Information

- Calories: 414.4
- Saturated Fat: 2
- Sodium: 652.8
- Fiber: 2.5
- Sugar: 0.4
- Total Carbohydrate: 73.2
- Cholesterol: 143.8
- Total Fat: 5.6
- Protein: 15.4

180. Swiss Steak In Foil

Serving: 5-6 serving(s) | Prep: 10mins | Ready in:

Ingredients

- 2 lbs round steaks, cut 1 ",thick
- 1 cup ketchup
- 1/4 cup flour
- 1 large onion, sliced thin
- 2 tablespoons lemon juice
- salt and pepper

Direction

- Tear off a 5' length of aluminum foil: fold double.
- Combine ketchup and flour.
- Spoon about 1/3 of mixture in center of foil, spreading slightly.
- Place steak on top of this.
- Season with salt and pepper.
- Cover meat with the onion slices, and remaining ketchup mixture.
- Sprinkle lemon juice over everything.
- Fold foil over and seal all edges securely.
- Place in a shallow baking pan, and bake at 450 for about 1 hr. or until meat is tender.

Nutrition Information

- Calories: 322.9
- Sodium: 630.1
- Sugar: 12.4
- Saturated Fat: 2.5
- Fiber: 0.8
- Total Carbohydrate: 20.4
- Cholesterol: 103.4
- Protein: 43.1
- Total Fat: 7.3

181. Swiss, Ham, Potato Soup

Serving: 4-6 serving(s) | Prep: 0S | Ready in:

Ingredients

- 2 medium potatoes, peeled diced
- 1/2 cup margarine
- 1/2 cup flour
- 2 green onions, chopped
- 2 -3 cups milk
- 4 slices swiss cheese
- 2 cups cooked ham, diced
- salt and black pepper

Direction

- Cook diced potatoes in saucepan with just enough water to cover.
- When tender, drain the liquid from the potatoes and save.
- Set both aside while making roux.
- In large saucepan, melt margarine.
- Saute the chopped green onions until tender.
- Remove onion from pan and set aside.
- Add flour to melted margarine and stir until incorporated.
- Cook over medium heat until the roux begins to just turn a golden color.
- Using a whisk, stir in 2 cups of milk and 1 cup of the saved potato liquid.
- Whisk until smooth and no lumps are seen.
- Bring just to a boil or until the soup thickens.
- Add the diced ham, cooked onion and the Swiss cheese. Also, add back in the cooked potatoes.
- Stir until cheese is melted.
- Add salt pepper to your preference.
- I usually add 1 teaspoons salt and 1/2 teaspoons pepper.
- Stir well.
- If soup is too thick, you may add the final cup of milk.
- My bunch likes it thick.

Nutrition Information

- Calories: 712.8
- Sodium: 427.9
- Sugar: 1.4
- Total Carbohydrate: 38.5
- Cholesterol: 106.3
- Protein: 33.8
- Saturated Fat: 16.1
- Fiber: 3
- Total Fat: 47.1

182. Three Colours Chocolate Crème

Serving: 6 serving(s) | Prep: 15mins | Ready in:

Ingredients

- 100 g plain dark chocolate
- 100 g white chocolate
- 100 g mocca milk chocolate with crunchy cocoa chips (or nibs. If you can't find a bar with the crunchy bits just use a plain mocha milk chocolate bar and)
- 2 eggs
- 3 dl milk
- 25 g sugar

Direction

- Break up each type of chocolate separately.
- Separate the eggs and place the egg whites in a measuring jug and keep in a cool place.
- Place the egg yolks in a bowl and stir.
- Heat the milk to boiling point, remove from the hob, and stir into the egg yolks.
- Pour everything back into the pan, and heat to boiling point, stirring all the while.
- Divide the crème into 3 portions. Dissolve one of each of the chocolate types into one each of the hot crème mixtures. Allow to cool.
- Beat the egg whites to a froth them gradually add the sugar to the beaten egg whites.
- Continue to beat until the mixture forms stiff peaks and is shiny.

- Fold the stiffly beaten egg whites in equal parts into the cooled chocolate mixtures. Place equal amounts of each chocolate in espresso coffee cups and keep cool until serving.

Nutrition Information

- Calories: 294.8
- Protein: 6.5
- Total Fat: 19.5
- Saturated Fat: 9.6
- Sodium: 112.9
- Sugar: 14.4
- Fiber: 3.7
- Total Carbohydrate: 30.1
- Cholesterol: 65.5

183. Two Colour Chocolate Terrine Panaché

Serving: 4 serving(s) | Prep: 7hours | Ready in:

Ingredients

- 100 g extra dark bittersweet chocolate (78 % cocoa)
- 100 g milk chocolate
- 1 egg
- 1/4 liter cream
- 2 teaspoons cognac or 2 teaspoons Amaretto
- raspberries, to decorate

Direction

- Rinse a 0.5 L terrine mould in cold water and line with cling film.
- Break up the two types of chocolate and melt them separately in the hot bain marie.
- Meanwhile, use the hand mixer to beat the egg into a lightly-coloured, thick, frothy mixture. Divide the mixture into two. Whip the cream until it is stiff.
- First carefully mix the liquid milk chocolate into half of the egg mixture. Add the cognac or Amaretto and fold in half of the whipped cream. Place into the prepared mould and place in the freezer for ten minutes. Mix the dark chocolate with the rest of the egg mixture and the cream in the same way, and pour onto the light chocolate. Cover, and keep in the refrigerator for a minimum of 6 hours to set.
- Turn out the terrine. Cut into thick slices and arrange with the raspberries.
- HINT. You can prepare the terrine the day before serving.

Nutrition Information

- Calories: 300.5
- Protein: 4.6
- Total Fat: 24.4
- Sodium: 54.8
- Fiber: 0.8
- Cholesterol: 108.9
- Saturated Fat: 14.9
- Sugar: 13
- Total Carbohydrate: 16.4

184. Ww 3 Points Swiss Miss Fat Free Chocolate Fudge Pudding

Serving: 4 serving(s) | Prep: 5mins | Ready in:

Ingredients

- 2 1/2 cups nonfat milk
- 2 tablespoons unsweetened cocoa powder
- 3 tablespoons cornstarch
- 1/2 cup sweetened evaporated skim milk
- 3 tablespoons Hersheys Chocolate Syrup
- 1 dash salt
- 1/2 teaspoon vanilla extract

Direction

- In a saucepan, combine the milk with the cocoa powder and cornstarch and whisk thoroughly until the powders are dissolved.
- Add the condensed milk, chocolate syrup, and salt to the saucepan. Set the pan over med/low heat. Heat the mixture, stirring constantly, until it comes to a boil and thickens (about 6 min).
- Remove from heat and let sit, covered, for about 5 minutes and then add the vanilla.
- Transfer into serving cups, cover each with plastic wrap and chill 2-3 hrs before serving.
- 3 Points per serving (3/4 cup).

Nutrition Information

- Calories: 148.3
- Total Fat: 0.9
- Saturated Fat: 0.5
- Sodium: 166.5
- Fiber: 1.3
- Cholesterol: 4.3
- Protein: 8.5
- Sugar: 18.5
- Total Carbohydrate: 27.2

185. Zupse Bread Swiss Bread

Serving: 10 serving(s) | Prep: 4hours | Ready in:

Ingredients

- 7 1/2 cups flour
- 7 tablespoons soft butter
- 2 2/3 cups scalded milk, cooled to lukewarm
- 4 teaspoons salt
- 1 teaspoon sugar
- 2 (1/4 ounce) packages yeast
- 1 egg

Direction

- Add the yeast to one cup of the scalded, cooled milk to proof.
- Mix the butter, sugar, salt and flour together.
- Beat the egg and add to the remaining milk.
- Make a well in the center of the flour mixture and add the milk/egg mixture.
- Mix well; add milk/yeast mixture.
- Mix well.
- Turn out of bowl and knead until no longer sticky.
- Replace in bowl, cover, and let rise until doubled.
- Punch down and let rise again until doubled.
- While dough is rising for the second time, preheat oven to 375°F.
- Form into loaves on a greased cookie sheet.
- Bake for approximately 35 minutes or bread sounds hollow when thumped.
- During the last ten minutes of baking, brush with an egg wash for a dark golden crust.

Nutrition Information

- Calories: 467.4
- Sodium: 1028.9
- Total Carbohydrate: 75.6
- Protein: 13.1
- Total Fat: 11.9
- Saturated Fat: 6.9
- Fiber: 2.8
- Sugar: 0.7
- Cholesterol: 51.6

Index

A
Almond 3,4,5,10,15,41,48,107
Apple 4,53,54,73
Asparagus 4,5,85,100,105

B
Bacon 3,4,5,20,24,25,26,63,64,82,88,90,95,103,107
Baking 89
Beef 3,9,33
Biscuits 4,48
Bran 5,88
Bread 4,5,54,66,67,108,112
Brie 93
Broccoli 3,9
Burger 4,5,80,102
Butter 13,19,28,41,61,76,78,93,95

C
Cabbage 3,18,33
Cake 3,4,28,40,44,49,50,56,58,76
Calvados 84
Caramel 44
Carrot 4,50
Cauliflower 3,7
Champ 5,94
Chard 3,4,5,6,26,27,29,31,32,34,35,36,43,77,78,94,96,104,106
Cheddar 3,20,82,96
Cheese 3,4,5,6,7,8,9,10,11,12,13,14,15,16,17,18,19,20,21,22,23,24,29,32,55,71,75,78,79,82,83,88,96,97,98,107
Cherry 3,4,19,55,61
Chicken 3,4,8,10,66
Chickpea 3,34,36
Chicory 4,63
Chocolate 3,4,5,38,41,44,48,50,55,56,76,82,86,87,88,91,92,93,101,110,111
Chutney 4,83
Cinnamon 4,64
Cocktail 5,84,106
Coffee 4,81,82
Cognac 69
Crab 3,9
Cranberry 4,79
Cream 3,4,5,23,27,44,48,61,62,63,88,94,106
Crisps 3,41
Cucumber 4,68
Curd 4,59
Custard 53

D
Date 3,42
Dijon mustard 19,21,23,27,51,63,70,77,84,100,105,108

E
Egg 3,19

F
Fat 3,5,6,7,8,9,10,11,12,13,14,15,16,17,18,19,20,21,22,23,24,25,26,27,28,29,30,31,32,33,34,35,36,37,38,39,40,41,42,43,44,45,46,47,48,49,50,51,52,53,54,55,56,57,58,59,60,61,62,63,64,65,66,67,68,69,70,71,72,73,74,75,76,77,78,79,80,81,82,83,84,85,86,87,88,89,90,91,92,93,94,95,96,97,98,99,100,101,102,103,104,105,106,107,108,109,110,111,112
Feta 3,34
Fish 5,106
Fontina cheese 84

French bread 23,69,70,83,84,108

Fudge 3,5,38,111

G

Garlic 4,5,63,64,104

Gin 4,47,87

Gouda 90

Gratin 4,73,78,82

Gravy 4,85

H

Ham 3,4,5,11,12,13,51,68,71,76,79,96,97,98,100,110

Hazelnut 4,48

Honey 3,4,39,56

I

Icing 40

J

Jus 42

K

Kirsch 4,61,62

L

Lard 5,103

Leek 4,78

Lemon 3,4,32,45,59

Liqueur 106

M

Macaroni 4,79

Marzipan 50

Meat 3,9

Meringue 4,57,80

Milk 4,5,57,91

Mozzarella 6

Muesli 3,4,5,42,73,101,108

Mushroom 3,4,5,15,30,72,80,94,102

Mustard 63

N

Nut 3,4,6,7,8,9,10,11,12,13,14,15,16,17,18,19,20,21,22,23,24,25,26,27,28,29,30,31,32,33,34,35,36,37,38,39,40,41,42,43,44,45,46,47,48,49,50,51,52,53,54,55,56,57,58,59,60,61,62,63,64,65,66,67,68,69,70,71,72,73,74,75,76,77,78,79,80,81,82,83,84,85,86,87,88,89,90,91,92,93,94,95,96,97,98,99,100,101,102,103,104,105,106,107,108,109,110,111,112

O

Oil 32

Olive 32

Onion 3,4,16,31,37,43,52,75,83,85

Orange 5,92

P

Pancakes 5,102

Pancetta 4,73

Parfait 5,107

Parmesan 3,6,7,12,13,16,25,28,71,96

Pasta 3,5,24,94

Pastry 53,60

Pear 4,44

Pecan 3,41

Peel 27,28,46,54,75

Pepper 3,5,8,43,101

Pie 4,60,98

Pineapple 4,79

Plum 4,58

Polenta 3,6

Port 3,15

Potato 3,4,5,12,13,25,26,28,30,32,36,43,71,73,75,76,77,82,98,103,110

Pulse 37

R

Raisins 3,34

Raspberry 4,5,48,92,106

Rice 3,7

Roquefort 64

S

Salad 4,63,64,68,76

Salt 27,29

Sausage 3,19

Savory 3,4,29,75

Scallop 3,25

Seasoning 35

Seeds 4,67

Soup 3,4,5,8,16,18,26,77,87,110

Spinach 3,5,16,27,90,95,97,106

Steak 4,5,72,85,99,109

Stew 3,36

Stuffing 3,8

Sugar
6,7,8,9,10,11,12,13,14,15,16,17,18,19,20,21,22,23,24,25,26,27,28,29,30,31,32,33,34,35,36,37,38,39,40,41,42,43,44,45,46,47,48,49,50,51,52,53,54,55,56,57,58,59,60,61,62,63,64,65,66,67,68,69,70,71,72,73,74,75,76,77,78,79,80,81,82,83,84,85,86,87,88,89,90,91,92,93,94,95,96,97,98,99,100,101,102,103,104,105,106,107,108,109,110,111,112

Swiss chard 6,26,27,31,32,43,77,94,96,104

Syrup 44,111

T

Tabasco 17

Tangerine 4,62

Tea 35,64,109

Terrine 5,111

Toffee 3,4,41,57

Tomato 3,4,14,29,36,83

Truffle 4,86,87

Turkey 5,97

V

Vegan 3,21

W

Walnut 4,60

Wine 3,4,21,69,70

Worcestershire sauce 17,18,20,29,51,52,72,99,100

Z

Zest 62

Conclusion

Thank you again for downloading this book!

I hope you enjoyed reading about my book!

If you enjoyed this book, please take the time to share your thoughts and post a review on Amazon. It'd be greatly appreciated!

Write me an honest review about the book – I truly value your opinion and thoughts and I will incorporate them into my next book, which is already underway.

Thank you!

If you have any questions, **feel free to contact at:** *author@hugecookbook.com*

Natasha Wu

hugecookbook.com

Manufactured by Amazon.ca
Acheson, AB